high up 1

Reinildes Dias
Doutora em Letras: Estudos Linguísticos pela Concordia University em Montreal, Canadá, Mestre em Letras – Inglês pela Universidade Federal de Minas Gerais (UFMG) e licenciada em Letras: Português-inglês pela Faculdade de Filosofia, Ciências e Letras de Sete Lagoas (Fundação Educacional "Monsenhor Messias"). É professora associada da Faculdade de Letras da UFMG e já atuou, por vários anos, como consultora da Secretaria da Educação (MG) e da Rede Municipal de Educação de Belo Horizonte (RME-BH). É autora da Proposta Curricular de Língua Estrangeira de Minas Gerais e coautora de Proposições Curriculares de Inglês da RME-BH.

Leina Jucá
Mestre em Letras: Estudos Linguísticos e licenciada em Letras pela Universidade Federal de Minas Gerais (UFMG). É professora assistente do Departamento de Letras da Universidade Federal de Ouro Preto, onde se dedica à formação inicial de professores de língua inglesa.

Raquel Faria
Mestre em Letras: Estudos Linguísticos e licenciada em Letras pela Universidade Federal de Minas Gerais (UFMG). Possui ampla experiência no ensino de língua inglesa e formação de professores. É consultora pedagógica nas redes pública e privada na área de ensino de línguas estrangeiras.

1ª edição
Cotia, SP – 2013

MACMILLAN

MACMILLAN

Diretora editorial: Ana Claudia Ferrari
Gerente editorial: Gisele Aga
Editora de arte: Simone Oliveira Vieira
Assistentes de arte: Carol Duran, Leticia Mantovani
Designer: Ivan Toledo Prado
Pesquisadora iconográfica: Gabriela Farcetta
Coordenadora de produto: Carla Rodrigues Riquena
Assistente de redação: Elena Regina Pucinelli
Coordenadora de produção gráfica: Roseli Said

Editoras de conteúdo: Carina Guiname Shiroma, Cecilia Skaf
Editor-assistente: Paulo Machado
Assistente editorial: Sybille Ariano
Preparadora: Adriana Bairrada
Revisoras técnicas: Patrizia Zagni, Thelma de Carvalho Guimarães
Revisor linguístico: Robert Caudle Garner
Projeto gráfico e capa: Simone Oliveira Vieira
Edição de arte e diagramação: Select Editoração
Ilustrações: Attílio, Mauro Souza
Iconografia: Gabriela Farcetta, Lipcia Mercado
Tratamento de imagens: Paulo César Salgado

Colaboradores
Simulados do Enem: Amini Rassoul, Avany Pazzani Chiaretti
***Self-study*:** Carla Maurício Vianna, Patrícia Muradas, Virgínia Galvão
***Spot Your Talent*:** Climene Arruda, Miriam Vieira, Vivian Margutti
***Glossary*:** João Rodrigo L. Agildo

Dados Internacionais de Catalogação na Publicação (CIP)
(Câmara Brasileira do Livro, SP, Brasil)

Dias, Reinildes
High Up: ensino médio / Reinildes Dias, Leina Jucá, Raquel Faria. -- Cotia, SP: Macmillan, 2013.

"Língua estrangeira moderna - Inglês" - Obra em 6 v.
ISBN 978-85-7418-908-6 (vol. 1, aluno)
ISBN 978-85-7418-911-6 (vol. 1, professor)
ISBN 978-85-7418-909-3 (vol. 2, aluno)
ISBN 978-85-7418-912-3 (vol. 2, professor)
ISBN 978-85-7418-910-9 (vol. 3, aluno)
ISBN 978-85-7418-913-0 (vol. 3, professor)

1. Inglês (Ensino médio) I. Jucá, Leina. II. Faria, Raquel. III. Título.

13-03622 CDD-420.7

Índices para catálogo sistemático:
1. Inglês: Ensino médio 420.7

MACMILLAN DO BRASIL
Rua José Félix de Oliveira, 383 – Granja Viana
Cotia – SP – 06708-645
www.macmillan.com.br
Atendimento ao professor: (11) 4613-2278
0800 16 88 77 (Outras regiões)
Fax: (11) 4612-6098

Impresso no Brasil - Silvamarts Gráfica e Editora - Outubro/2014

Apresentação

Prezado(a) aluno(a),

Bem-vindo(a) ao **High Up**! Para você compreender a coleção que apoiará seu aprendizado de inglês, o melhor é, primeiro, entender seu título.

High Up quer dizer "em uma posição destacada e de prestígio", "no topo", "com um status diferenciado". Assim, é o lugar que podem ocupar aqueles que são bilíngues por se comunicarem em língua materna e em inglês com competência. Frequentemente, é uma posição que abre as portas para oportunidades diferenciadas na universidade e no trabalho.

Como indica o título, esta coleção tem o objetivo de contribuir para que você passe a desempenhar uma posição de destaque por compreender e expressar-se bem na língua inglesa, nesta era da colaboração em rede e do conhecimento construído interdisciplinarmente. A coleção visa a proporcionar oportunidades para que você amplie seus conhecimentos sobre si mesmo(a), sobre sua própria cultura e sobre outras culturas pelo mundo, apropriando-se de saberes para se posicionar criticamente diante de questões pessoais, sociais e profissionais de seu dia a dia, local e globalmente.

Você, prezado(a) aluno(a), é o(a) principal agente desta coleção. Por isso, cada unidade começa pelo que você tem a dizer. Seu conhecimento de mundo e suas opiniões são extremamente importantes para fazê-lo(a) compreender e produzir textos multimodais, orais e escritos, dos mais diversos gêneros textuais, e utilizar letramento digital nas situações de aprendizado do inglês, muitas vezes em conjunto com outras disciplinas do currículo. Ao longo da coleção, você vai ainda aplicar estratégias de aprendizagem, ampliar seu vocabulário e fazer escolhas para aprender melhor. Para aprofundar seu conhecimento gramatical, você analisará e estudará exemplos dos textos que lê, ouve, fala e escreve sempre dentro do seu contexto real. Enfim, a coleção **High Up** fornece o suporte necessário para que você construa seu próprio conhecimento ao aplicá-lo, consolidá-lo e avaliá-lo em contextos diversos na sua vida pessoal e na escolar.

Enquanto aprende inglês, você desenvolverá autonomia, exercendo seu protagonismo, o que lhe poderá ser útil por toda a vida. Para fornecer-lhe o apoio necessário neste processo, a coleção valoriza e incentiva o uso de vários recursos tecnológicos para a aprendizagem, o trabalho colaborativo com seus colegas, o aprendizado além dos limites da sala de aula, a consolidação dos aspectos textuais, léxicos e gramaticais para aprender mais, as pesquisas on-line e em material impresso, tendo em vista um olhar interdisciplinar. Ao final de cada aula, esperamos que você sinta que está em busca de uma posição de destaque por ser capaz de ler, escrever, ouvir e falar em inglês ao encarar os desafios da vida contemporânea, agora e no futuro. *Go further with* ***High Up!***

As autoras

Conheça seu livro.

AS UNIDADES DO LIVRO SÃO ORGANIZADAS POR SEÇÕES. CONHEÇA UM POUCO MAIS SOBRE ELAS A SEGUIR.

ABERTURA

Contém imagens que irão colocá-lo em contato com o tema da unidade, juntamente com perguntas que o levarão a explorar essas fotos. Além disso, traz um resumo de tudo o que você estudará na unidade.

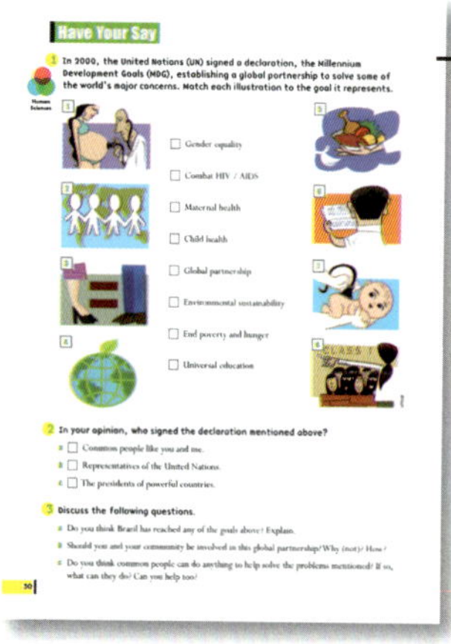

HAVE YOUR SAY

Abre espaço para que você diga o que pensa sobre determinados assuntos. Propicia que você discuta sobre alguns tópicos e ative o conhecimento que você já tem sobre as questões abordadas na unidade.

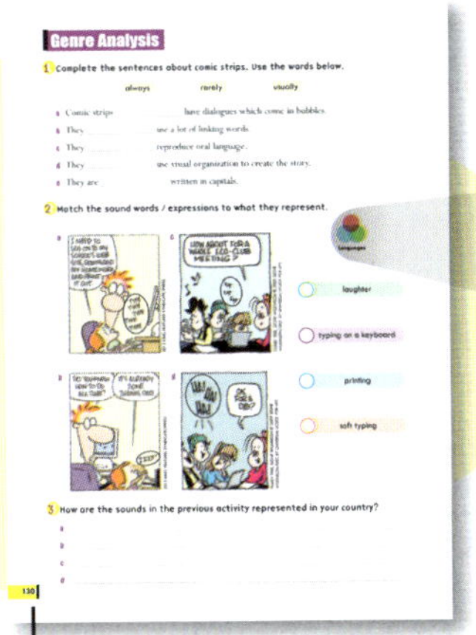

Representa a relação interdisciplinar com outras áreas de conhecimento.

READING BEYOND THE WORDS

Desafia você a ler e interpretar textos de diversos gêneros – artigos, reportagens, histórias em quadrinhos, *quizzes*, questionários etc.

GENRE ANALYSIS

Permite que você explore as características básicas dos gêneros escritos e orais da unidade.

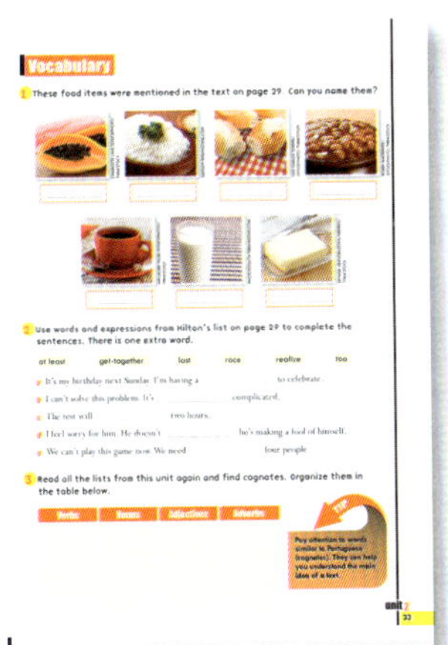

VOCABULARY

Promove o estudo contextualizado do vocabulário ligado à seção **Reading Beyond the Words**.

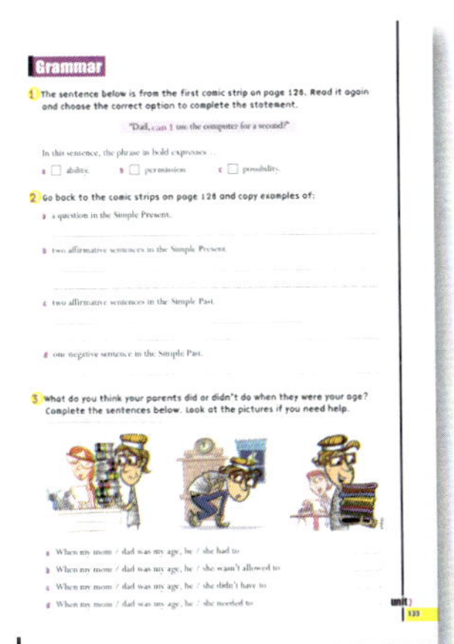

GRAMMAR

Permite que você desenvolva seu conhecimento gramatical por meio de atividades contextualizadas pelo gênero e assunto do texto da seção **Reading Beyond the Words**.

IN OTHER WORDS

Fornece explicações em português de aspectos gramaticais presentes nos gêneros de cada unidade. Deve ser tida como referência nos seus estudos de inglês.

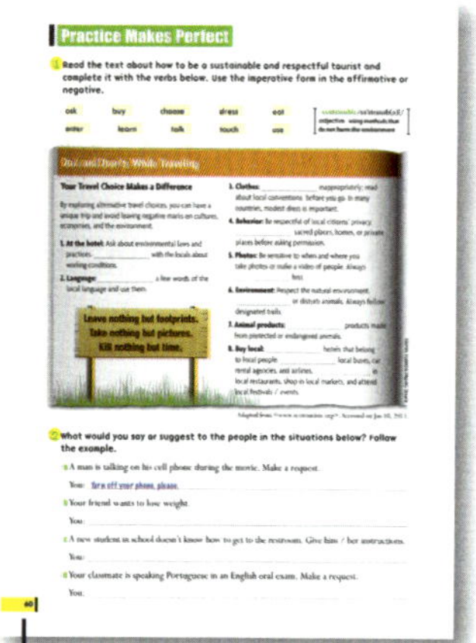

PRACTICE MAKES PERFECT

Oferece a você novas oportunidades de praticar itens gramaticais presentes nos gêneros de cada unidade.

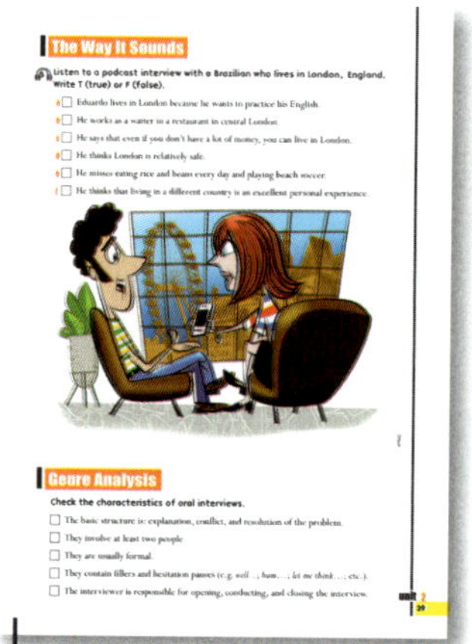

THE WAY IT SOUNDS

Ajuda você a desenvolver a sua compreensão oral por meio de diversos gêneros relacionados aos temas das unidades.

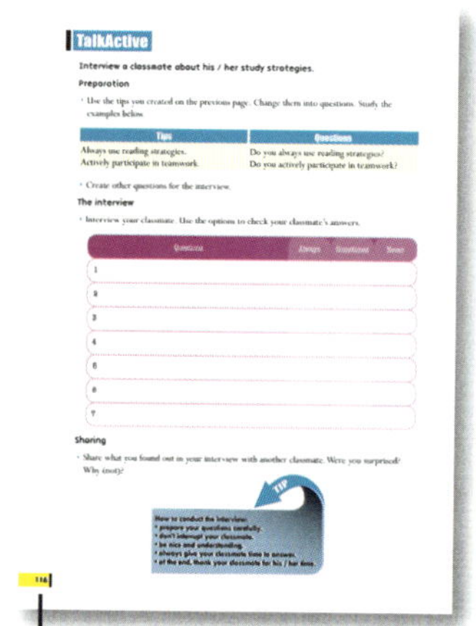

TALKACTIVE

Ajuda você a desenvolver a sua capacidade de comunicar-se oralmente em inglês. Além disso, o incentiva a assumir uma posição crítica em relação aos assuntos abordados nesta seção.

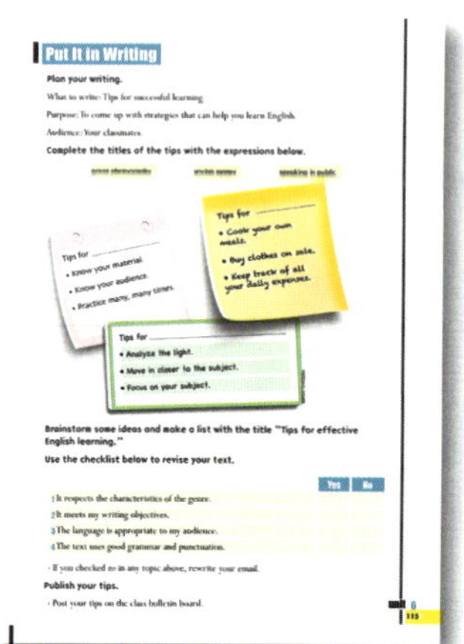

PUT IT IN WRITING

Facilita o desenvolvimento da sua capacidade de produzir textos em inglês, levando em conta seu propósito, seu público-alvo e as características do seu gênero.

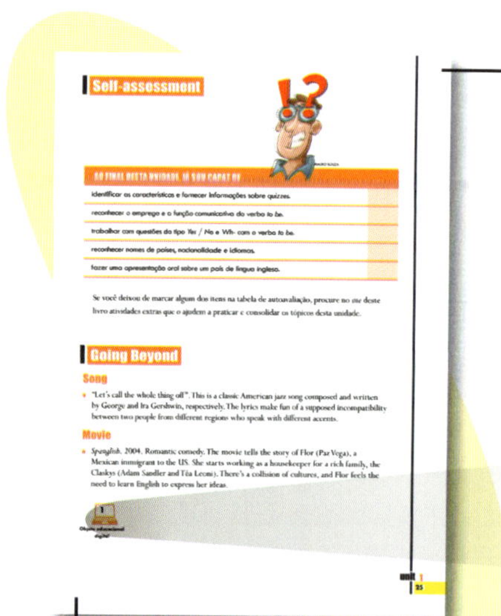

GOING BEYOND

Apresenta opções diversificadas – músicas, vídeos, programas de TV e *sites* – para você aprender inglês fora da sala de aula.

SELF-ASSESSMENT

Oferece oportunidades para você avaliar seu próprio progresso de aprendizagem de inglês nas unidades estudadas.

Objeto educacional digital

Representa o objeto educacional digital disponível na unidade.

ALÉM DAS UNIDADES, O LIVRO TRAZ ALGUMAS SEÇÕES ESPECIAIS QUE REFORÇAM O SEU APRENDIZADO.

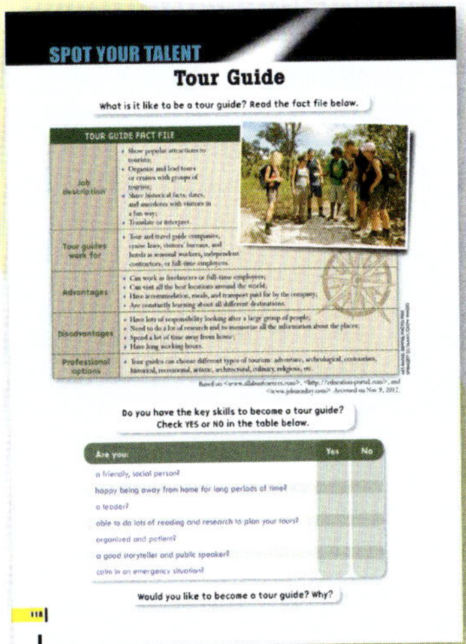

SPOT YOUR TALENT

Na primeira página desta seção, são exploradas diferentes profissões, com o objetivo de estimular a sua reflexão sobre possíveis escolhas de futuras carreiras. Na segunda página, há um trabalho de produção escrita relacionado ao mundo profissional.

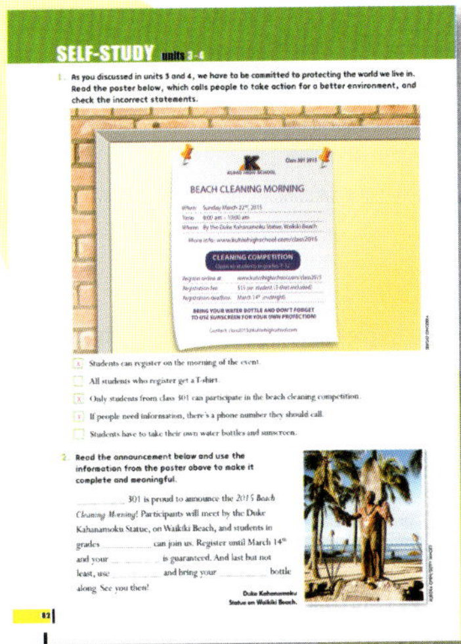

SELF-STUDY

Tem como objetivo incentivá-lo a estudar sozinho para consolidar a aprendizagem do que você estudou ao longo das unidades.

GLOSSARY

Traz definições de palavras encontradas nos textos e nas atividades de cada unidade. Abre espaço também para que você construa o seu próprio glossário. Ao final, há uma lista de verbos irregulares para consultar sempre que precisar.

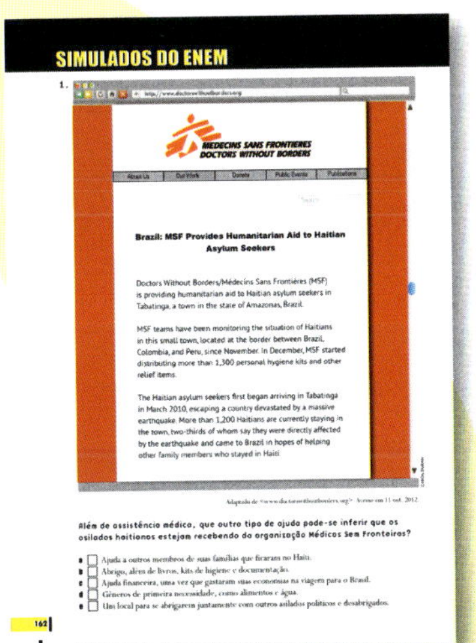

SIMULADOS DO ENEM

Traz atividades similares às do ENEM, com o objetivo de familiarizá-lo com o formato dessa avaliação.

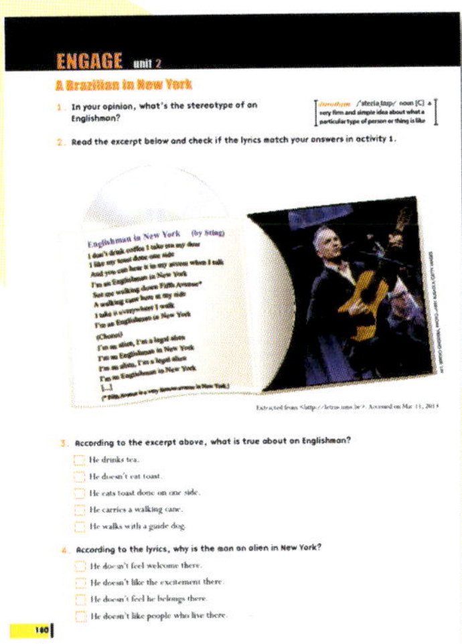

ENGAGE

Apresenta atividades desafiadoras que incentivarão a sua autonomia no processo de aprender inglês.

CONTENTS

OPÇÃO BRASIL IMAGENS

ENGLISH EVERYWHERE

NESTA UNIDADE VOCÊ IRÁ:

- identificar as características de *quizzes*;
- usar o verbo *to be*;
- trabalhar com questões do tipo *Yes* / *No* e *Wh-* com o verbo *to be*;
- reconhecer nomes de países, nacionalidades e idiomas;
- fazer uma apresentação oral sobre um país de língua inglesa.

PHOTO RESEARCHERS RM/GETTY IMAGES

unit 1

ISTOCKPHOTO/THINKSTOCK

- Em que medida o inglês está presente no Brasil? Cenas como a retratada na página anterior são comuns onde você vive?
- Que aspectos dos países onde se fala inglês estão representados nas imagens desta página?

Have Your Say

1 Write the names of the countries in the correct place.

Human Sciences

Australia · Canada · England · Guyana · India

Jamaica · Kenya · Nigeria · Philippines · South Africa

1 USA

2 ____________

3 Ireland

4 ____________

5 Singapore

6 ____________

7 ____________

8 ____________

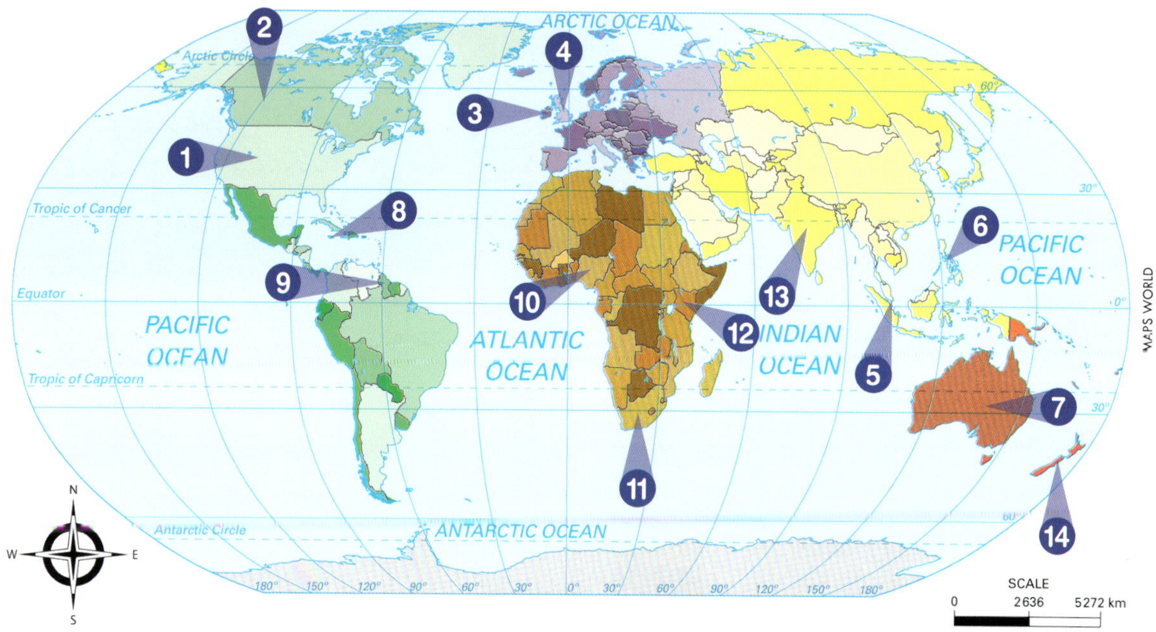

Based on *Atlas geográfico escolar*. Rio de Janeiro: IBGE, 2009. p. 32.

9 ____________

10 ____________

11 ____________

12 ____________

13 ____________

14 New Zealand

2 What do these countries have in common?

____

Did you know?

Nowadays, American English is very influential because of the USA's dominance of cinema, television, popular music, trade, and technology (including the Internet). However, there are many other varieties of English around the world, including Australian English, Canadian English, South African English, Indian English, and others.

3 Look at this scene from a Brazilian city and discuss with a classmate. Which of these English words do you see around your neighborhood? Are they common?

MAURO SOUZA

4 Make a list of English words or expressions we use in Brazil. Write them under the appropriate category.

Clothing	Food	Sports	Technology

5 Discuss the questions below.

a Why is the English language so important in the contemporary world?

b Do you remember a situation when you had to speak English? If so, describe it.

c How does the English language help you in your daily life?

6 Some of the countries on the map on the previous page speak more than one language. Match the languages below to the countries where they are spoken.

a Afrikaans ☐ Canada

b Filipino ☐ South Africa

c French ☐ India

d Guyanese Creole ☐ Philippines

e Hindi ☐ Guyana

Reading Beyond the Words

[**quiz** /kwɪz/ noun [C] a short oral or written test that is frequently taken without preparation]

1 Take a quick look at the quiz below. What is it about?

____

2 Take the quiz and check your results.

Trivia Quiz

Test your knowledge of English-speaking countries and the English language.

Currency of South Africa

City of Auckland

1 Which is the currency (monetary unit) in South Africa?
a [ ] The African dollar, divided into 100 cents.
b [ ] The rand, divided into 100 cents.
c [ ] The cedi, divided into 100 pesewa.

2 Which is the only English-speaking country in South America?
a [ ] Guyana.
b [ ] Barbados.
c [ ] Suriname.

3 Which is the most popular sport in Canada?
a [ ] Ice hockey.
b [ ] Soccer.
c [ ] Cricket.

4 The words “shampoo”, “coffee”, and “tea” come from other languages. Which are their original languages?
a [ ] Swahili, Mandarin, and Portuguese.
b [ ] Hindi, Arabic, and Chinese.
c [ ] Japanese, French, and Vietnamese.

5 Kingston is the capital city of which country?
a [ ] South Africa.
b [ ] Jamaica.
c [ ] Trinidad and Tobago.

6 Where is the city called Auckland located?
a [ ] In England.
b [ ] In Australia.
c [ ] In New Zealand.

7 What is special about Chaucer’s poems?
a [ ] They are written in Modern English.
b [ ] They are written in Middle English.
c [ ] They are written in Old English.

8 Which country doesn’t border Belize?
a [ ] Nicaragua.
b [ ] Mexico.
c [ ] Guatemala.

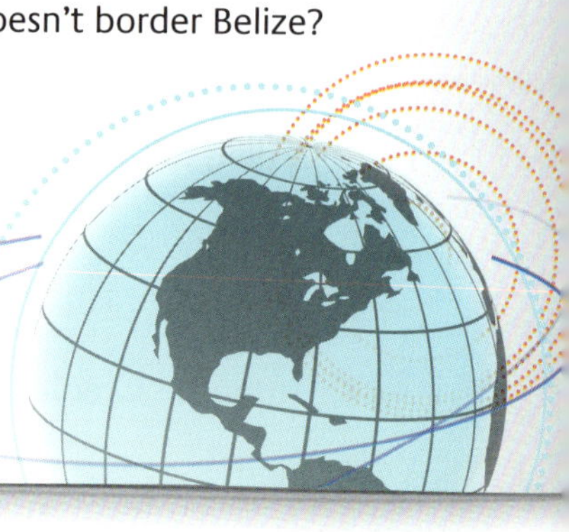

6 Teen World

Geoffrey Chaucer with a book, from The Canterbury Tales, Herman Scheerre, c.1410

City of Montreal

9 What percentage of the Internet is in English, approximately?

a [ ] 86%.
b [ ] 92%.
c [ ] 99%.

10 Which country won its independence from Britain in 1957?

a [ ] Fiji.
b [ ] Sierra Leone.
c [ ] Ghana.

11 Which language besides English is spoken in Canada?

a [ ] Spanish.
b [ ] French.
c [ ] Hindi.

12 According to the US Census, how many languages are spoken in the United States?

a [ ] Over 300.
b [ ] Under 300.
c [ ] About 200.

Results:

- If you had **11** to **12** correct answers, congratulations! Your knowledge of English-speaking countries and the English language is excellent!
- If you had **08** to **10** correct answers, well done! Look up the information you don't know, and you will surely do better next time!
- If you had **05** to **07** correct answers, try harder. There's still a long way to go, but you can do it!
- If you had **04** or **fewer** correct answers, watch out! You might not be paying as much attention as you should to the world around you.

Answers: 1 b, 2 a, 3 a, 4 b, 5 b, 6 c, 7 b, 8 a, 9 a, 10 c, 11 b, 12 a

Based on <www.englishclub.com> and <world-english.org>. Accessed on Oct 13, 2012.

ART: RAFAEL GENTILE/ROBERTA BENITES; PHOTOS: CLIFF PARNELL/ISTOCKPHOTO/THINKSTOCK (1); DMITRYP/DREAMSTIME.COM (2); THE BRITISH LIBRARY (3); ISTOCKPHOTO/THINKSTOCK (4)

Genre Analysis

1 Check the characteristics that define a quiz.

a ☐ It is usually published in the entertainment section of a magazine, newspaper, or website.

b ☐ It is usually organized either in questions or in incomplete statements.

c ☐ It is usually written in a fixed sequence: introduction, development, and conclusion.

d ☐ It is usually well designed and illustrated to catch the reader's attention.

e ☐ It is usually preceded by a general question to challenge the reader to answer it.

f ☐ It usually brings a result based on the number of correct answers the reader may have.

2 Research about the countries below, and create three new multiple-choice questions for the quiz. Use your questions to test your classmates.

a

IBGE

Ireland

☐ ______

☐ ______

☐ ______

b

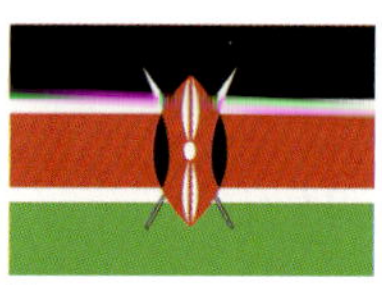

IBGE

Kenya

☐ ______

☐ ______

☐ ______

c

IBGE

Singapore

☐ ______

☐ ______

☐ ______

3 Share your quiz questions with the class.

Vocabulary

1 Study the dictionary entries. Then circle the country and underline the nationality in the short conversation below.

[**country** /ˈkʌntri/ noun [C] an area of land that has its own government and official borders]

[**nationality** /ˌnæʃəˈnæləti/ noun [C/U] the legal status of being a citizen of a particular country]

A: Where are Murilo Benício and Débora Falabella from?

B: They're from Brazil. They're Brazilian.

2 Match the columns.

a Indian people are from ☐ Switzerland.

b German people are from ☐ Denmark.

c Swiss people are from ☐ India.

d Danish people are from ☐ Italy.

e Italian people are from ☐ Germany.

3 Unscramble the letters to find names of countries.

a OTUHS FAICRA ________________

b GIRENIA ________________

c BLAZRI ________________

d SAUTIARAL ________________

4 Write the nationality that corresponds to each country to complete the table below. Use a dictionary if necessary.

-ish	-an / -ian	-ese	others
Ireland ________	Canada ________	Japan ________	New Zealand ________
England ________	Jamaica ________	Portugal ________	France ________
Spain ________	USA ________	China ________	Greece ________

5 Answer these questions.

a Where are you from? ________________

b What are your parents' nationalities? ________________

Grammar

1 Unscramble the words to form affirmative sentences.

a America / country / located / This / North / is / in

____

b speak / English / there / French / People / and

____

c Ottawa / city / The / is / capital

____

d constitutional / The / government / monarchy / form / of / is

____

e unit / The / the / monetary / dollar / is

____

2 The sentences in activity 1 are about a country. Which country is it? ______________

3 Read some facts about New Zealand and circle the forms of the verb *to be*.

Cool facts about New Zealand

1. A kiwi is not a fruit – it is New Zealand's native bird and a nickname for New Zealanders.
2. Queen Elizabeth II is officially the queen of the country. She is represented in New Zealand by a Governor General.
3. New Zealand has two official national anthems. They are "God Save the Queen" (the English National Anthem) and "God Defend New Zealand".
4. There are approximately nine sheep to every human in New Zealand.

ART: RAFAEL GENTILE; ILLUSTRATION: MAURO SOUZA

Adapted from <listverse.com>. Accessed on Oct 18, 2012.

4 Complete the questions with the correct form of the verb *to be* and answer them.

a What ______________ your name? ______________________________

b How old ______________ you? ______________________________

c Where ______________ you from? ______________________________

d What ______________ your address? ______________________________

5 Match the two columns to organize a conversation between two girls.

a Who is this guy? | ☐ He's from Curitiba.
b Is he a soccer player? | ☐ He's Anderson Silva.
c What is his nickname? | ☐ I think he's 40 or over.
d Where is he from? | ☐ He's "The Spider".
e How old is he? | ☐ No, he's an MMA fighter.

JOE CORRIGAN/GETTY IMAGES

6 Ask questions about important cities in the world.

MICHAEL JUNG/DREAMSTIME.COM

a A: ____________________

B: Cape Town is in Africa.

FHINNIG/DREAMSTIME.COM

b A: ____________________

B: Brasília is more than 50 years old.

SWISSSTOCK/DREAMSTIME.COM

c A: ____________________

B: It's La Paz.

SCANRAIL/DREAMSTIME.COM

d A: ____________________

B: Yes, the Danish are the people from Denmark.

EFIRED/DREAMSTIME.COM

e A: ____________________

B: They're from Thailand.

7 Find out where five classmates are from.

Name	Origin

In Other Words

Verbo *to be*

Lembre-se de que o verbo *to be*:

- tem conjugação irregular; sua forma varia de acordo com o sujeito da frase.
- geralmente liga o sujeito a alguma qualidade, denominação ou estado:

> *Qualidade:* Ice hockey **is** popular in Canada.
> *Denominação:* I **am** a teacher.
> *Estado:* They **are** happy.

- é também usado como verbo auxiliar:

> Auckland **is** situated in New Zealand.
> They **are** flying to Kenya right now.

- possui formas completas (como nos exemplos anteriores) e abreviadas:

> Ice hockey**'s** the most popular sport in Canada.
> We**'re** learning about English language and culture.
> I**'m** a quiz freak.

As frases afirmativas seguem esta sequência: sujeito + verbo. As negativas acrescentam o *not* após o verbo.

> I**'m not** Brazilian.
> Toronto **isn't** the capital of Canada.

As frases interrogativas são formadas pela inversão: primeiro o verbo *to be*, depois o sujeito.

MONKEY BUSINESS IMAGES/DREAMSTIME.COM

ANDRESR/DREAMSTIME.COM

Wh-questions

Fazemos perguntas para buscar informações. Assim, se queremos saber o local e a data de um evento, perguntamos *onde* e *quando* ele vai acontecer. Em inglês, para fazer muitas dessas perguntas usamos pronomes interrogativos conhecidos como *wh-words*, por isso elas são chamadas de ***wh-questions***.

Wh-word	Usado para perguntar sobre...	Exemplo
How	maneira ou modo.	**How** do you go to school?
How many	quantidade para substantivos contáveis.	**How many** books do you carry in your schoolbag?
How much	quantidade para substantivos incontáveis.	**How much** water do you drink every day?
How often	a frequência com que algo é feito ou acontece.	**How often** do you see your grandparents?
What	coisas, ações, ideias.	**What** do they normally do after class?
When	tempo.	**When** are you going to study for the test?
Where	locais.	**Where** do you live?
Which	um item específico de um grupo.	**Which** color do you prefer: red or purple?
Why	razões.	**Why** do you want to learn English?

Observe que *how* também é usado antes de adjetivos:

How old are you?
How big is your schoolbag?

Practice Makes Perfect

1 Write sentences to say the nationalities of the celebrities below. Follow the example.

a Rihanna

b Sebastian Vettel

c Penélope Cruz

d Cristiano Ronaldo

e Prince Henry and Prince William

a *Rihanna is Barbadian.*

b ____________________

c ____________________

d ____________________

e ____________________

2 Read the extract from an interview with Gisele Bündchen published in *GQ* magazine. Fill in the blanks with the correct form of the verb *to be*.

GQ: Can you remember the last time someone took advantage of you?

GB: Look, I know who I ______ and where I ______ from. I think there is danger obviously when you ______ really young and they make you all glamorous and you start thinking you ______ that, but you ______ only playing a role. The important thing for me ______ that I never believed... This ______ exactly how I describe my work: I get there, I put on the clothes, I model, I leave them on the hanger, and I go home. And that ______ what I do.

GQ 15

ART: RAFAEL GENTILE; PHOTO: STEPHANE CARDINALE/PEOPLE AVENUE/CORBIS/LATINSTOCK

Adapted from <abcnews.go.com>. Accessed on Oct 13, 2012.

3 Write questions for the sentences below.

a ____________________

I'm nineteen years old.

b ____________________

I'm from Cuiabá.

c ____________________

It's in Mato Grosso.

d ____________________

Yes, I am and I'm also a swimmer.

The Way It Sounds

1 Listen to the letters of the alphabet and repeat them.

🎧 2

a b c d e f g h i j k l m
n o p q r s t u v w x y z

2 Listen to the spelling of some countries and write their names.

🎧 3

a ____________________ d ____________________

b ____________________ e ____________________

c ____________________

> **spelling** /ˈspelɪŋ/ noun [C] sequence of letters that compose a word

3 Listen to a radio quiz show. Number the countries in the order you hear them. There is one extra country.

🎧 4

☐ Australia

MRALLEN/DREAMSTIME.COM

☐ Belize

MARK WEBSTER/LONELY PLANET IMAGES/GETTY IMAGES

☐ England

JONATHAN LARSEN/ISTOCKPHOTO/THINKSTOCK

☐ Ghana

JANE HAHN/GETTY IMAGES

☐ Ireland

NOEL MOORE/HEMERA/THINKSTOCK

TalkActive

Present your favorite English-speaking country.

- Choose your favorite English-speaking country.
- Research about it. Use your school library, magazines, books, and the Internet.
- Find the following pieces of information and complete the summary below.

Complete name: ________________________________.

Colors of the flag: ________________________________.

Famous people from this country: ________________________________.

National symbol: ________________________________.

Population: ________________________________.

Capital: ________________________________.

Largest city: ________________________________.

Internet domain: ________________________________.

Monetary unit: ________________________________.

Popular dish: ________________________________.

Popular festival(s) or celebration(s): ________________________________

________________________________.

CAROL DURAN

- Prepare what you are going to say in your presentation. Use full sentences.

  The colors of the flag of my English-speaking country are black, gold, green, white, red, and blue.
- Present your country to the class, but keep its name a secret. Can your classmates guess what your favorite English-speaking country is?

Self-assessment

MAURO SOUZA

AO FINAL DESTA UNIDADE, JÁ SOU CAPAZ DE

identificar as características e fornecer informações sobre *quizzes*.
reconhecer o emprego e a função comunicativa do verbo *to be*.
trabalhar com questões do tipo *Yes* / *No* e *Wh-* com o verbo *to be*.
reconhecer nomes de países, nacionalidade e idiomas.
fazer uma apresentação oral sobre um país de língua inglesa.

Se você deixou de marcar algum dos itens na tabela de autoavaliação, procure no *site* deste livro atividades extras que o ajudem a praticar e consolidar os tópicos desta unidade.

Going Beyond

Song

- "Let's call the whole thing off" (George and Ira Gershwin). The lyrics make fun of a supposed incompatibility between two people from different regions who speak with different accents.

Movie

- *Spanglish*. 2004. Romantic comedy. The movie tells the story of Flor (Paz Vega), a Mexican immigrant to the US. She starts working as a housekeeper for a rich family, the Claskys (Adam Sandler and Téa Leoni).

Websites

- Listen to news from other English-speaking countries and notice the different English varieties: Australian <www.abc.net.au/news/video/>; Belizean <http://blip.tv/belize>; Canadian <www.cbc.ca/player/News/>; Indian <www.ndtv.com/video/live/channel/ndtv24x7>; Irish <www.independent.ie/videos/>; Jamaican <http://jamaica-gleaner.com/videos/>; South African <www.sabc.co.za/news/radio_tv>.

1
Objeto educacional digital

PETER ADAMS/PHOTOLIBRARY/GETTY IMAGES

BRAZIL: OUR PEOPLE, OUR COUNTRY

NESTA UNIDADE VOCÊ IRÁ:

- refletir sobre alguns estereótipos a respeito dos brasileiros;
- estudar palavras relacionadas a comidas e hábitos brasileiros;
- trabalhar com os gêneros lista e entrevista oral;
- usar o *Simple Present*;
- identificar e utilizar *adverbs of frequency*.

TONY QUINN/ICON SMI/CORBIS/LATINSTOCK

unit 2

JEREMY WOODHOUSE/PHOTODISC/GETTY IMAGES

- A que aspectos da cultura brasileira essas imagens se relacionam?
- Qual dessas imagens melhor representa a cultura da região onde você vive? Por quê?

Have Your Say

Human Sciences

1 Below are some statements about Brazil. Check the ones you agree with. Discuss your answers with a classmate.

a ☐ It's the land of soccer, which is played and loved by everyone.

b ☐ Child labor is still a serious social problem in our country.

c ☐ Brazilians are friendly to tourists who come on their vacation.

d ☐ Most Brazilians still face poor living conditions nowadays.

2 Read the definition of stereotype. Discuss if any of the sentences above express one.

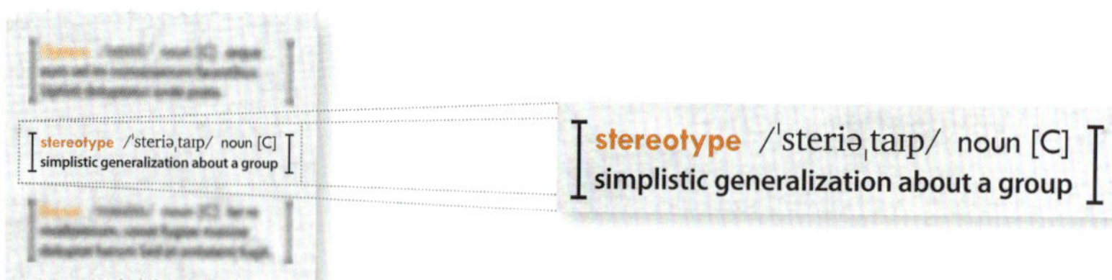

3 Classify the sentences below into the two categories. The first one is done for you.

A – stereotypes of American people

B – stereotypes of British people

DRAGHICICH/DREAMSTIME.COM

ANJELAGR/DREAMSTIME.COM

a [B] They always carry an umbrella.

b ☐ They eat a lot of junk food.

c ☐ They are very patriotic.

d ☐ They drink tea at 5 o'clock.

e ☐ They are very materialistic.

f ☐ They are always punctual.

4 Do you know any other stereotypes? Make a list in your notebook and discuss it with your class.

Reading Beyond the Words

1 Complete the clause below with your ideas.

You know you're Brazilian when…

- ____
- ____
- ____
- ____

2 Read the text below and check the author's ideas that are similar to yours.

www.meetup.com

blog

Login Find:

Home | Members | Sponsors | Photos | Discussions | More ▼ | Join us

New York, NY

About us...

Brazilians and Friends 250
Group Members 423
Photos
Our Calendar
More

New York City Brazilians

Posted May 16, 2012 2:43 PM — Link to this discussion

You know you're Brazilian when...

- your entire family goes to grandma's house on Sundays for a big family get-together;
- you can name at least 30 *novelas* and 10,000 actors / actresses;
- you travel to Brazil and take presents for the entire family, the dog, the neighbors, etc.;
- you can dance;
- you take soccer too seriously;
- you know the difference between *samba* and *pagode*;
- you eat rice and beans (or you would love to) 7 days a week;
- your breakfast consists of milk and coffee, bread and butter, and maybe a piece of papaya;
- you are so used to corruption that nothing surprises you anymore;
- you don't care about race or color. And once you come to the US, you realize what racism means;
- you know how to party, and if the party doesn't last until after 5 am... it's not a party;
- you are too friendly.

Hilton

Adapted from <www.meetup.com>. Accessed on Sep 27, 2012.

3 Check the appropriate answers about the text on the previous page.

a What text genre is this?

- [ ] An article.
- [ ] A list.
- [ ] A quiz.

b What's its objective?

- [ ] To give an opinion about Brazilians.
- [ ] To disapprove of Brazilians.
- [ ] To defend Brazilians.

4 Scan the list on the previous page to answer the questions below.

a Where was it taken from?

____

b Who's the author?

____

c When was the list published?

____

d Where does the author probably live?

____

TIP

When you read a text quickly to get its general idea, you are using the *skimming* strategy. If you read it quickly to find specific information, you are using the *scanning* strategy.

5 Group the items in Hilton's list into these three headings.

Eating habits	Personal characteristics	Social habits
You eat rice and beans (or you would love to) 7 days a week.	You can dance.	Your entire family goes to grandma's...

6 Write T (true) or F (false), according to the information in Hilton's list on page 29.

A ◯ Brazilians frequently visit their families.

B ◯ Brazilians dislike TV soap operas.

C ◯ Brazilians take soccer more seriously than they should.

D ◯ Brazilians don't like to party.

E ◯ Brazilians eat rice and beans (or would love to) every day.

ART: ERIKA ONODERA; PHOTOS: JACK HOLLINGSWORTH/THINKSTOCK (1); PURESTOCK/THINKSTOCK (2); RATMANDUDE/DREAMSTIME.COM (3); JUPITERIMAGES/GOODSHOOT RF/THINKSTOCK (4); AIDA RICCIARDIELLOCABALLERO/ISTOCKPHOTO/THINKSTOCK (5)

7 Read the list again and discuss the questions below with a classmate.

a Which ideas are positive?

b How do the negative ideas make you feel?

c Among Hilton's opinions, which one(s) do you agree with? Why?

d Which of his opinions do you disagree with? Why?

e Do you think the author gives a stereotypical view of Brazilians? Why (not)?

Genre Analysis

list /lɪst/ noun [C] a set of names, numbers, etc. that are written or printed one below another

1 **Here are some characteristics of a list. Which ones apply to Hilton's?**

a ☐ There is usually a sequence of items or topics.

b ☐ It may be a sequence of instructions (*Go to the corner, turn left, stop at the light.*).

c ☐ It usually uses numbers or bullets to separate the items.

d ☐ It does not use discourse markers (*so*, *then*, *and*, *additionally*, etc.) to connect items.

e ☐ It can be of various types (opinion topics, recipe ingredients, things to do, etc.).

2 **Match each title below to its list. Compare your answers with a partner.**

a shopping list **c** to do list

b list of objectives **d** playlist

TIP

Lists differ from each other according to their content, authorship, intended audience, organization of items, and layout.

☐
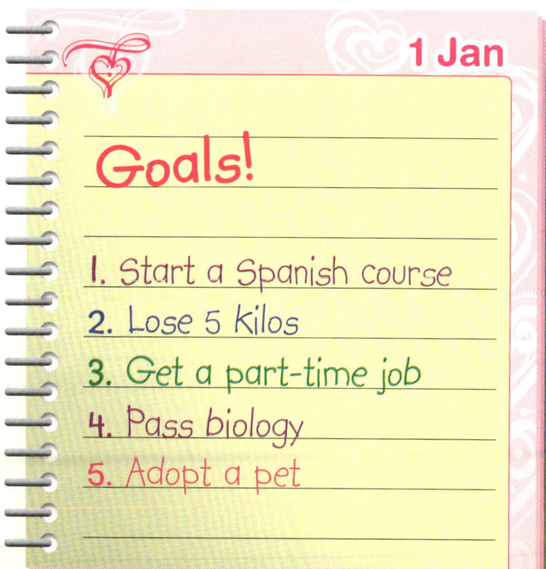

☐
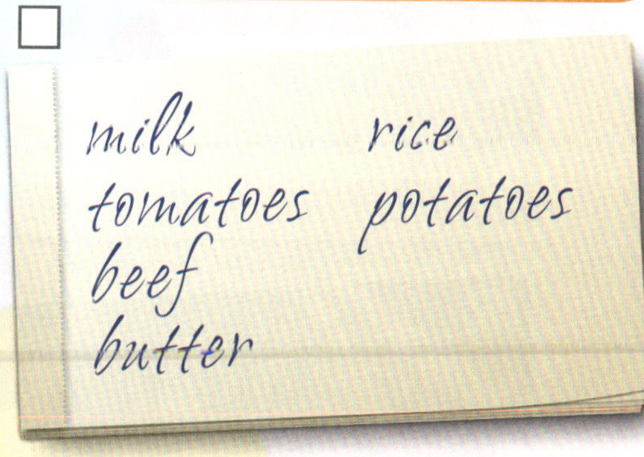

☐

☐
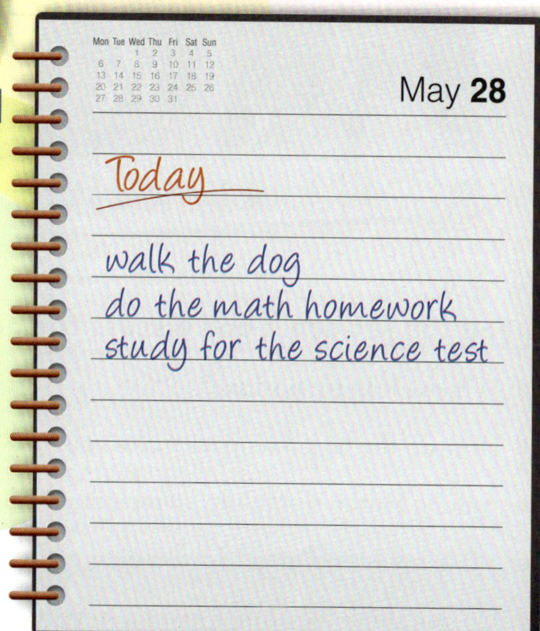

RAFAEL GENTILE

Vocabulary

1 These food items were mentioned in the text on page 29. Can you name them?

CHARLOTTE LAKE/ISTOCKPHOTO/THINKSTOCK

ILDIPAPP/DREAMSTIME.COM

LUIS CARLOS TORRES/ISTOCKPHOTO/THINKSTOCK

ROBIN MACKENZIE/ISTOCKPHOTO/THINKSTOCK

WELLFORD TILLER/ISTOCKPHOTO/THINKSTOCK

PHOTOSTOUCH/DREAMSTIME.COM

LILYANA VINOGRADOVA/HEMERA/THINKSTOCK

2 Use words and expressions from Hilton's list on page 29 to complete the sentences. There is one extra word.

at least   get-together   last   race   realize   too

a It's my birthday next Sunday. I'm having a ______________ to celebrate.

b I can't solve this problem. It's ______________ complicated.

c The test will ______________ two hours.

d I feel sorry for him. He doesn't ______________ he's making a fool of himself.

e We can't play this game now. We need ______________ four people.

3 Read all the lists from this unit again and find cognates. Organize them in the table below.

Verbs	Nouns	Adjectives	Adverbs

TIP

Pay attention to words similar to Portuguese (cognates). They can help you understand the main idea of a text.

Grammar

1 Underline the verbs in the statements about Brazilian people below.

a Your entire family goes to grandma's house on Sundays.

b You travel to Brazil and take presents for the entire family.

c You take soccer too seriously.

d You eat rice and beans seven days a week.

e Your breakfast consists of milk and coffee.

2 The verbs in activity 1 are in the...

☐ present. ☐ past. ☐ future.

3 The Simple Present expresses different ideas. Look at the mind map below and do the activities.

a Cross out the ideas that are not expressed by the Simple Present.

b Match the statements from activity 1 with the ideas in the diagram. The first one is done for you.

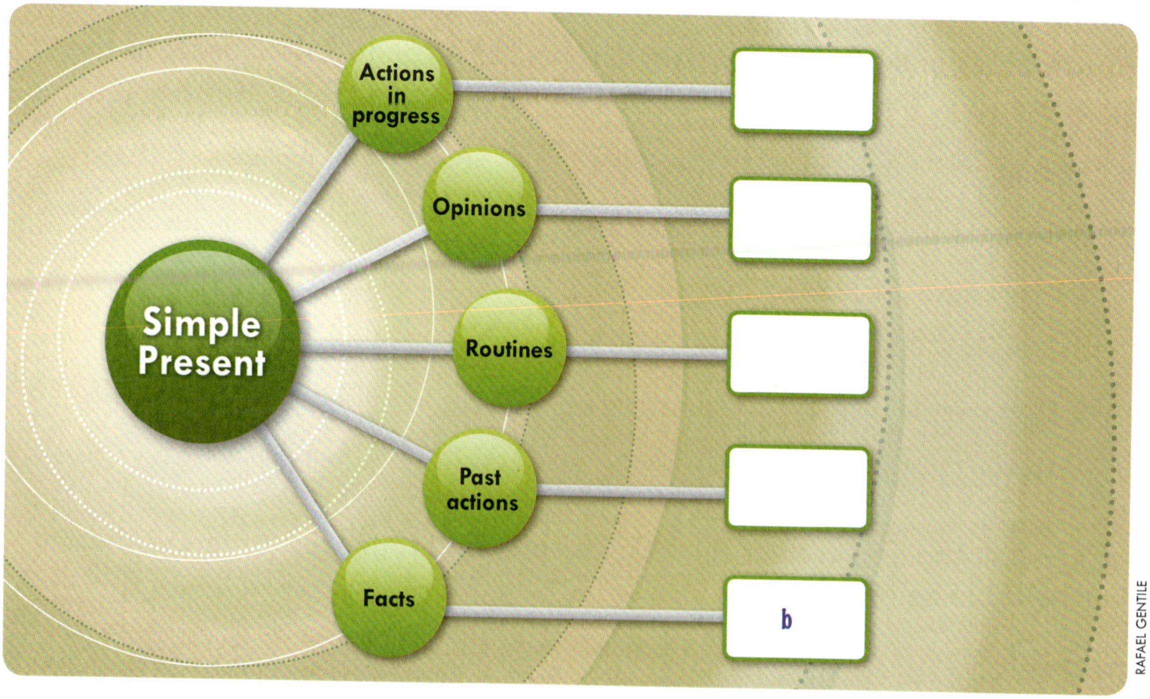

RAFAEL GENTILE

4 Go back to page 29. Find three sentences with verbs in the Simple Present and write them down.

____

____

____

In Other Words

Presente (*Simple Present*)

Significado:

O *Simple Present* é normalmente usado para expressar ideias relacionadas a:

- hábitos (coisas que as pessoas fazem normalmente e / ou repetidamente).

Your entire family **goes** to grandma's house on Sundays.

My grandmother never **has** lunch alone on Sundays.

JACK HOLLINGSWORTH/THINKSTOCK

- fatos / verdades em geral.

Vegetarians **don't eat** meat.
Brazilian people **speak** Portuguese.

Forma:

Usa-se o verbo em sua forma básica para todas as pessoas, exceto a terceira pessoa do singular. Para formá-la, na maioria dos casos, acrescenta-se *-s*:

put – put**s**
work – work**s**

Em verbos terminados em *-o*, *-s*, *-x*, *-z*, *-sh*, *-ch*, acrescenta-se *-es*:

go – go**es**
wash – wash**es**

Quando o verbo termina em consoante seguida de *-y*, retira-se o *-y* e acrescenta-se *-ies*:

cry – cr**ies**
study – stud**ies**

Do e *does* são verbos auxiliares usados em sentenças negativas, interrogativas e respostas curtas.

My family **doesn't** watch soap operas every day.

Do you take soccer too seriously?
No, I **don't**.

Adverbs of Frequency

Significado:

Ao falar de ações habituais ou repetitivas, é comum nos referirmos à frequência com que as praticamos. Para isso, utilizamos os *adverbs of frequency*. Veja, no quadro abaixo, a frequência expressa por alguns dos advérbios mais comumente usados.

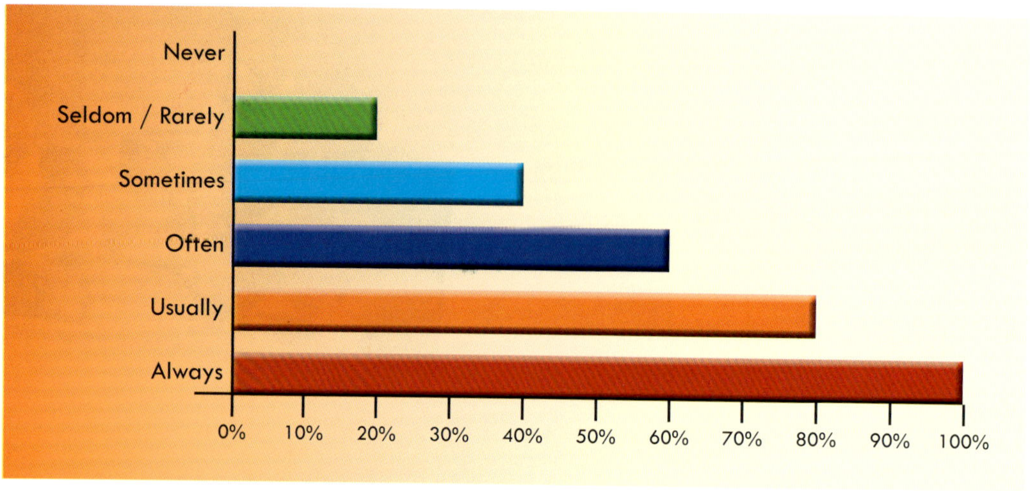

ROBERTA BENITES

Forma:

Os advérbios de frequência vêm depois do verbo *to be*.

I'm **never** late.
She isn't **always** so friendly.

Em frases afirmativas com outros verbos, os advérbios de frequência vêm normalmente entre o sujeito e o verbo principal.

I **usually** have lunch with my family on Sundays.

Em sentenças negativas, os advérbios ficam entre o verbo auxiliar e o verbo principal.

He doesn't **usually** drink coffee.
They don't **often** go to the movies.

Practice Makes Perfect

1 Complete the list of ten things Diane hates about soap operas. Choose from the verbs below.

answers are are drink eat goes
happen has is needs wear

a The stories __________ very predictable.

b Women __________ makeup 24 hours a day.

c People's hair __________ always neat and clean.

d All men __________ strong and show their muscles.

e Nobody __________ to go to the bathroom.

f Nobody __________ a stomachache.

g Unbelievable coincidences __________ all the time.

h People never really __________ or __________ anything.

i The villain never __________ to jail.

j The phone is never busy and somebody always __________ it.

BANANASTOCK RF/THINKSTOCK

2 Rewrite the statements about your habits, using the adverbs.

a I go home for lunch. I have lunch near school. (never, often)

____

b I don't eat rice and beans. I eat soy. (usually, sometimes)

____

c My boyfriend has lunch with me. His mother cooks for him. (rarely, always)

____

3 Look at the diagram on page 36 and then use the adverbs of frequency to write sentences that are true about you.

Example: I never go to school on foot. I always take a bus.

a ______________________________

b ______________________________

c ______________________________

d ______________________________

e ______________________________

Put It in Writing

Plan your writing.

What to write: A list of your personal habits related to the traditions of the state where you live.

Purpose: To show which state traditions you follow and which ones you don't.

Audience: Your classmates, teachers, coordinators, and family.

Study some examples. Guess the state of each writer. The first one is done for you.

a

- I have "tacacá" almost every week, but I only eat "pato no tucupi" on special occasions.
- I dance "carimbó," and I like to watch people dancing too.

a Pará ______

b

- I never eat "pão de queijo," but I love "broa de fubá."
- I rarely go swimming in waterfalls.

b ______

c

- I have "chimarrão" every day.
- I am a vegetarian, so I don't eat barbecue.

c ______

ARTS: ROBERTA BENITES

Brainstorm some of your state's traditions and take notes in your notebook. Then write a list of your own habits related to those traditions.

Use the checklist below to revise your text.

	Yes	No
1 It respects the characteristics of the genre.		
2 It meets my writing objectives.		
3 The language is appropriate to my audience.		
4 The text uses good grammar and punctuation.		

- If you checked *no* in any topic above, rewrite your list.

Publish your list.

The Way It Sounds

5 Listen to a podcast interview with a Brazilian who lives in London, England. Write T (true) or F (false).

a ☐ Eduardo lives in London because he wants to practice his English.

b ☐ He works as a waiter in a restaurant in central London.

c ☐ He says that even if you don't have a lot of money, you can live in London.

d ☐ He thinks London is relatively safe.

e ☐ He misses eating rice and beans every day and playing beach soccer.

f ☐ He thinks that living in a different country is an excellent personal experience.

ATTÍLIO

Genre Analysis

Check the characteristics of oral interviews.

☐ The basic structure is: explanation, conflict, and resolution of the problem.

☐ They involve at least two people.

☐ They are usually formal.

☐ They contain fillers and hesitation pauses (e.g. *well*...; *hum*...; *let me think*...; etc.).

☐ The interviewer is responsible for opening, conducting, and closing the interview.

TalkActive

Interview a classmate about his / her habits in relation to the common traditions in her / his state.

Preparation

- Read a personal list of habits created by one of your classmates.
- Write questions to understand better why he / she has his / her habits.

RAFAEL GENTILE

- Study the characteristics of an interview.
- Prepare an introductory and a closing message.

The interview

- Make sure you have all the material to record the interview (camera, audio recorder, or pen and paper).
- Follow the plan you prepared before.
- Give your interviewee time to answer the questions. (Don't interrupt!)

Sharing

- Role-play your interview.

Self-assessment

MAURO SOUZA

AO FINAL DESTA UNIDADE, JÁ SOU CAPAZ DE	
analisar criticamente alguns estereótipos sobre brasileiros.	
estudar palavras relacionadas ao Brasil, a seu povo e a sua culinária.	
identificar características e intenção comunicativa do gênero lista.	
identificar características e intenção comunicativa de entrevistas orais.	
reconhecer o emprego e a função comunicativa do *Simple Present*.	
identificar e utilizar *adverbs of frequency*.	

Se você deixou de marcar algum dos itens na tabela de autoavaliação, procure no *site* deste livro atividades extras que o ajudem a praticar e consolidar os tópicos desta unidade.

Going Beyond

Movies

- *Gonzaga – De pai para filho*. 2012. Drama. The story of a father and son in the *sertão* of Brazil's northeast.
- *Xingu*. 2012. Drama. Brothers Orlando (Felipe Camargo), Cláudio (João Miguel), and Leonardo Villas Bôas (Caio Blat) trade the comfort of living in a big city for the adventure in exploring the forests of Brazil.

2

Objeto educacional digital

DJ

What is it like to be a DJ? Take a look at the mind map below.

DISC JOCKEY – DJ

- Uses special equipment: plates, mixers, microphones, amplifiers.
- Uses different formats: vinyl, CD, MP3.
- **Types of DJs**
  - Club DJ
    - Plays and mixes records in clubs or bars.
    - Operates lighting and visual effects.
    - Manipulates rhythm, effects, and samples to produce new sounds.
  - Mobile DJ
    - Freelancer
    - Brings equipment and music to special events.
  - Radio DJ
    - Presenter
      - Selects the music.
      - Interacts with the audience.
      - Interviews guests.
    - Weather Reader
    - Announcer
    - Newscaster

PROS	CONS
training and experience beyond high school	competitive area
many radio personalities earn a lot	special event DJs and club DJs have only part-time income
most of the ordinary radio DJs have a reasonable income	long and irregular working hours
opportunities for beginners in smaller radio stations	possibility of drinking a lot and / or committing illegal activities, if regularly working in night events
	must wear earplugs or eardrums may burst

RAFAEL GENTILE

Adapted from <www.getmeacooljob.com>. Accessed on Nov 9, 2012.

Do you have the key skills to become a DJ? Check YES or NO in the table below.

Do you have:	Yes	No
a strong interest in music?		
a confident and extroverted personality?		
a clear speaking voice (for radio work)?		
a good sense of timing?		
knowledge of technical equipment?		
the ability to improvise and think quickly?		
the ability to operate different equipment at the same time?		

Would you like to become a DJ? Why?

FACT FILES (part I)

A **fact file** is a collection of significant facts related to a specific event, person, or place.

Read the fact file about volunteer work and check its characteristics below.

VOLUNTEER WORK

HILL STREET STUDIOS/ERIC RAPTOSH/BLEND IMAGES/GETTY IMAGES

A volunteer serves the society, promoting good or improving quality of life for certain communities or groups of people, usually without financial benefits. Volunteers can work individually or in organizations, within specific areas (such as education or environmental issues) or in emergency situations (when natural disasters occur, for example).

Benefits	• It's an opportunity to change lives. • It develops skills that can be used later in the workplace. • It's a way to socialize and meet new people. • It brings personal growth and sense of respect.
Some volunteering ideas	• Implementing a recycling program at your school or in your community. • Joining an organization against teen violence. • Mentoring. • Donating to or helping at charity institutions. • Working at summer camps.

Based on <http://voices.yahoo.com>. Accessed on Nov 9, 2012.

Fact files:

- [ ] express personal opinions about a specific subject.
- [ ] bring key facts about a specific event, person, or place.
- [ ] are written in long paragraphs.
- [ ] are a fictional narrative.
- [ ] inform people about a specific subject.
- [ ] are organized in topics.

1. Take this trivia quiz about international celebrities. Refer back to page 16 to review its basic characteristics. It is also a good idea for you to go back to pages 18 and 21 to revise how questions are formed.

Quiztime!

Who are they?

1

A. She is a British writer. She is the author of the *Harry Potter* series.

- [ ] Virginia Woolf
- [ ] J.K. Rowling
- [ ] E. L. James

2

B. He is an American satirist and animator. He is the creator of The Simpsons.

- [ ] Matt Groening
- [ ] Stephen King
- [ ] George Clooney

3

C. He is well-known Canadian actors.

- [ ] Michael J. Fox
- [ ] Will Smith
- [ ] Hugh Jackman

4

D. He is an Italian tenor and musician.

- [ ] José Carreras
- [ ] Andrea Bocelli
- [ ] Plácido Domingo

5

E. She is a famous South African actress.

- [ ] Meryl Streep
- [ ] Angelina Jolie
- [ ] Charlize Theron

F. He is an Argentinian soccer player.

- [ ] Cesc Fàbregas
- [ ] Lionel Messi
- [ ] Clarence Seedorf

6

38 | STARS!

ART: SERGIO ONODERA; PHOTOS: BEN PRUCHNIE/GETTY IMAGES (1); FRANK MICELOTTA/PICTUREGROUP/AP IMAGES/GLOW IMAGES (2); KEVIN WINTER/GETTY IMAGES (3); JIN YI BJ/IMAGECHINA/AP PHOTO/GLOW IMAGES (4); JOEL RYAN/AP PHOTO/GLOW IMAGES (5); MANU FERNANDEZ/AP PHOTO/GLOW IMAGES (6)

2. The verb to be is one of the most important verbs in English and also one of the most frequently used.
Fill in the blanks with the correct form of the verb to be and notice its use in the quotations that follow. Refer back to Unit 1 to learn more about this verb and to see its use in different contexts. Take the chance to also review pages 18 and 20.

a The love of one's country __________ a splendid thing. But why should love stop at the border?

(Pablo Casals – Catalan cellist and conductor)

b Nothing and no one can destroy the Chinese people. They __________ relentless survivors.

(Pearl S. Buck – American writer)

c It __________ a well-known fact that we always recognize our homeland when we __________ about to lose it.

(Albert Camus – French writer)

d Experience __________ what happens to you; it'__________ what you do with what happens to you.

(Aldous Huxley – English writer)

e It'__________ what you look at that matters; it'__________ what you see.

(Henry David Thoreau – American writer and poet)

f I __________ an Athenian or a Greek, I am a citizen of the world.

(Socrates – Greek philosopher)

Extracted from <www.brainyquote.com> and <http://quotationsbook.com/>. Accessed on Jan 17, 2013.

3. Questions and answers are very important for communication to take place. In English, we use wh-questions to get information about facts, people, places, time, things, etc. Refer back to pages 21 and 22 to review the wh-questions and how to use them appropriately in social interactions. Then match the questions on the left to the answers on the right to learn more about how to use wh-questions for communicative purposes.

a Who is that girl?	☐ We're fine, thanks.
b What does he do?	☐ There are twenty.
c Which cap do you prefer, the green or the red one?	☐ She is my best friend.
d Where do you live?	☐ I live in the suburbs.
e When is he coming?	☐ I think he is a teacher.
f Why is the baby crying?	☐ Once a month.
g How are you?	☐ Just a little.
h How often do you go to the theater?	☐ The green one.
i How much coffee do you drink?	☐ On Friday morning.
j How many children are there in Joan's class?	☐ Because she can't sleep.

4. Verbs are very important in written or oral texts. They are usually defined as words which show action or a state of being. Verbs help us understand the meaning of a message. Refer back to pages 34 and 35 to learn more about verbs in the Present tense.
Read Karen's set of opinions about the TV series *The Vampire Diaries*. She explains why she loves it. Choose the right verb forms in parentheses to complete her opinions.

a. Paul Wesley and Ian Somerhalder ______________________ (is / are) handsome actors who ______________________ (plays / play) the roles of Stefan and Damon Salvatore wonderfully. Actually, the show ______________________ (has / have) an amazing cast!

b. The town of Mystic Falls ______________________ (is / are) the perfect setting for secrets upon secrets.

c. The show entertains, touches, and ______________________ (scares / scare) us at the same time.

d. Major events ______________________ (happens / happen) every week and we ______________________ (keeps on / keep on) looking forward to watching the following episode.

e. We ______________________ ever ______________________ (doesn't... get / don't... get) bored with the fantastic soundtrack.

ART: SERGIO ONODERA; PHOTO: CHELSEA LAUREN/WIREIMAGE/GETTY IMAGES

5. In our everyday lives, whenever we talk about our routine, we usually refer to the frequency we do activities. Adverbs of frequency are used to express more detailed information about the frequency we do our activities.
Read the statements below and choose the correct option to make them complete and meaningful.

a I hate milk. I ______________ drink it.
- [ ] always
- [ ] never
- [ ] often

b He drinks tea two or three ______________ a week.
- [ ] times
- [ ] once
- [ ] twice

c We love pizza, but we don't ______________ eat it because we're on a diet.
- [ ] always
- [ ] twice a day
- [ ] how often

d People say Americans ______________ a lot of junk food.
- [ ] doesn't eat
- [ ] eats
- [ ] eat

e It is said that Brazilians ______________ about race or color.
- [ ] doesn't care
- [ ] don't care
- [ ] cares

6. Go back to page 17 to review vocabulary about nationalities. Read the sentences below and complete them.

CORY SCHWARTZ/GETTY IMAGES

a His name's Bono Vox and he's from Ireland. He's ________________.

ROBERT MARQUARDT/WIREIMAGE/GETTY IMAGES

b Her name's Laura Pausini and she's from Italy. She's ________________.

GIULIO MARCOCCHI/SIPA/AP IMAGES/GLOW IMAGES

c He is Javier Bardem and he's from Spain. He's ________________.

ADRIAN WYLD/THE CANADIAN PRESS/AP PHOTO/GLOW IMAGES

d She is Shakira and she's from Colombia. She's ________________.

JIN SHUO/IMAGECHINA/AP IMAGES/GLOW IMAGES

e He is Maradona and he's from Argentina. He's ________________.

7. Read Anna's to-do list and take the opportunity to improve your knowledge of this text genre. Refer back to page 32 to review its basic characteristics.
Read Anna's to-do list again and complete it with the verbs below to make it complete and meaningful.

make   pick up   put away   take   water

________________ Darren, Joel, and Noah at school.
________________ dirty clothes to the laundry.
________________ the plants.
________________ the clean dishes.
________________ soup for dinner.

dishes (noun): louça
laundry (noun): lavanderia
pick up (phrasal verb): pegar, buscar
put away (phrasal verb): guardar
water (verb): regar

✔ Check your answers on page 208.

CULTURA RF/GETTY IMAGES

DON'T WASTE TIME AND TAKE ACTION NOW

NESTA UNIDADE VOCÊ IRÁ:

- trabalhar com um texto de convocação;
- refletir sobre a desigualdade no posicionamento de mulheres e homens;
- usar diferentes formas de se referir a datas;
- usar a forma imperativa dos verbos;
- discutir sobre as contribuições pessoais para a melhoria das condições de vida no planeta.

ISTOCKPHOTO/THINKSTOCK

unit 3

NAVARRORAPH/DREAMSTIME.COM

- Que tipos de ações para melhorar o mundo estão representadas nas imagens?
- Você já viu alguma destas iniciativas na sua comunidade?

Have Your Say

1 In 2000, the United Nations (UN) signed a declaration, the Millennium Development Goals (MDG), establishing a global partnership to solve some of the world's major concerns. Match each illustration to the goal it represents.

Human Sciences

1
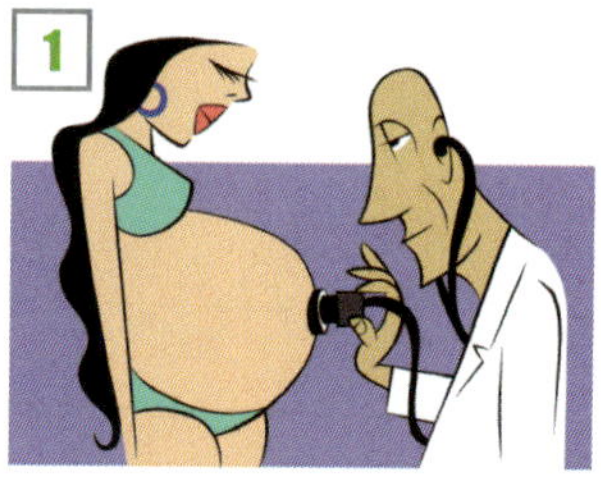

2

3
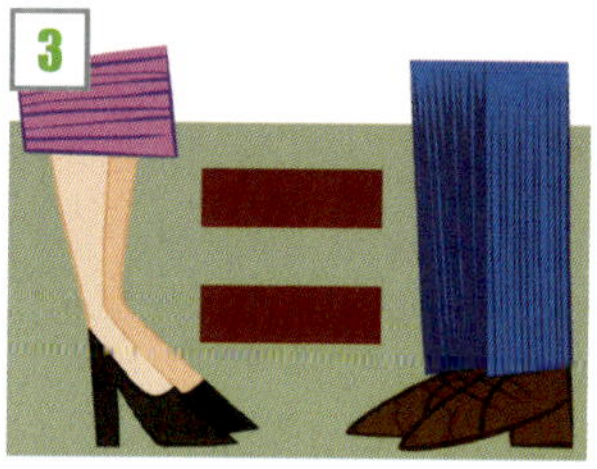

4

- ☐ Gender equality
- ☐ Combat HIV / AIDS
- ☐ Maternal health
- ☐ Child health
- ☐ Global partnership
- ☐ Environmental sustainability
- ☐ End poverty and hunger
- ☐ Universal education

5

6
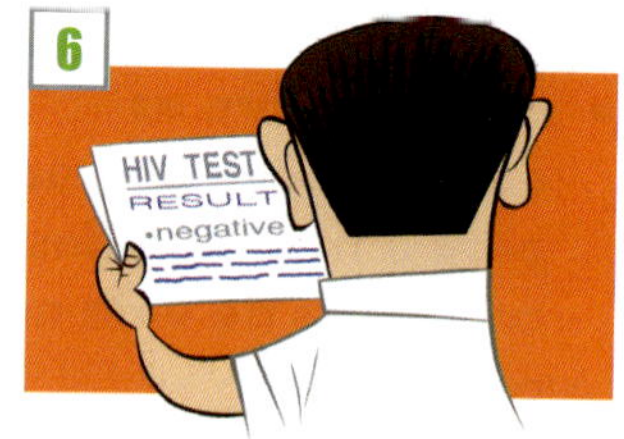

7
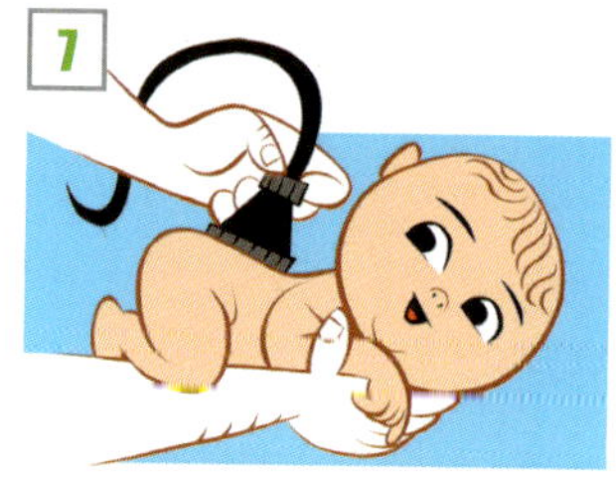

8

ATTÍLIO

2 In your opinion, who signed the declaration mentioned above?

a ☐ Common people like you and me.

b ☐ Representatives of the United Nations.

c ☐ The presidents of powerful countries.

3 Discuss the following questions.

a Do you think Brazil has reached any of the goals above? Explain.

b Should you and your community be involved in this global partnership? Why (not)? How?

c Do you think common people can do anything to help solve the problems mentioned? If so, what can they do? Can you help too?

Reading Beyond the Words

1 Look at the icons in the Learn section of the website below. What do they represent? Then read the Share and the Act sections as well.

____

____

http://www.worldwewant2015.org

Home | About | The Process | Consultations | Contact Us | Login | Register

Learn | Share | Act

In **2000** our leaders decided to halve extreme poverty by **2015**

We have made great progress, but 1.4 billion people still live in poverty. Inequality is growing and our planet is at risk.

Together we can save people and planet.

Learn | **Share** | Act

Join the Global Conversation! Contribute to shaping the post-2015 development agenda!

This is an opportunity to discuss the issues we care about most and build a sustainable future by the people and for the people. Share your ideas, provide your suggestions, and encourage others to join the conversation on **www.worldwewant2015.org.**

Learn | Share | **Act**

In partnership with civil society, the **United Nations** is coordinating over 50 country consultations and more than eight thematic consultations (Inequalities, Governance, Growth and Employment, Health, Education, Environmental Sustainability, Food Security and Nutrition, Conflict and Fragility, Population Dynamics, Energy, Water). Add your voice to these initiatives here:

Enter your email address to register.

SignUp

RAFAEL GENTILE

Adapted from <www.worldwewant2015.org>. Accessed on Oct 28, 2012.

2 Check the objective of the text you have just read.

a ☐ To invite people to participate in a project.

b ☐ To describe the purpose of a website.

c ☐ To share the results of a campaign.

3 Check the correct alternative to complete the sentences below.

a In 2000, it was decided poverty should be reduced by:

☐ 100%.

☐ 25%.

☐ 50%.

b 1.4 billion is the number of people who:

☐ no longer live in poverty.

☐ helped to eradicate poverty.

☐ still live in poverty.

c WorldWeWant2015.org is the website to be used to:

☐ evaluate the problems of the project.

☐ share ideas and provide suggestions.

☐ vote for the goals to be achieved.

d 50 is the number of countries:

☐ the UN intends to hold consultations with.

☐ with the most serious global problems.

☐ in which civil society is providing solutions.

e Your email address is required to:

☐ enlarge the number of participants.

☐ receive further information.

☐ register and participate.

4 Think about the world you want for the future and discuss the following questions with a classmate.

a How could you contribute today to the Global Conversation?

b What can you, your friends, and your family do to improve life in your community?

5 Read the essay below and check the issue it illustrates.

essay /ˈeseɪ/ noun [C] a short piece of writing on a particular subject that is published in a book, magazine, or newspaper

a ☐ homosexual segregation

b ☐ child health

c ☐ gender in inequality

I want a wife!

by Judy Brady

I belong to that classification of people called wives. I am A Wife. And, not incidentally, I am a mother.

Not long ago, a male friend announced his recent divorce. He had one child, who is, of course, with his ex-wife. He is looking for another wife. As I thought about him while I was ironing one evening, it occurred to me that I, too, would like to have a wife. Why do I want a wife?

I would like to go back to school so that I can become economically independent. I want a wife who will work and send me to school. And while I am going to school, I want a wife to take care of my children.

I want a wife who will keep my house clean. A wife who will pick up after my children, a wife who will pick up after me. I want a wife who will keep my clothes clean, ironed, mended, replaced when necessary, and who will keep my personal things in their proper place so that I can find what I need the minute I need it.

If, by accident, I find another person more suitable as a wife than the wife I already have, I want the liberty to replace my present wife. Naturally, I will expect a fresh new life; my ex-wife will take the children and be responsible for them so that I am free.

When I finish school and have a job, I want my wife to quit working and stay home so that my wife can more fully and completely take care of a wife's duties.

My God, who *wouldn't* want a wife?

25 | The Modernist

CAROL DURAN

Adapted from <www.columbia.edu> (originally published in *Ms. Magazine*, 1971). Accessed on Oct 28, 2012.

6 Circle the alternative that correctly completes each sentence about the text.

a The author is a **woman** / **man**.

b The tone of the essay is **serious** / **ironic**.

c One of the author's arguments is that women **do too much** / **should do more**.

d The author is showing how **men see women** / **women see themselves**.

e The author wants the reader to **ignore the situation**/ **take action**.

7 The text on the previous page uses literary resources to emphasize ideas. Match each figure of speech with an example from the text.

Languages and Human Sciences

a Irony: saying the opposite of what you mean to add humor.

b Hyperbole: exaggeration.

☐ "I want a wife who will keep my clothes clean, ironed, mended, replaced when necessary, and who will keep my personal things in their proper place so that I can find what I need the minute I need it."

☐ "My God, who *wouldn't* want a wife?"

☐ "... I, too, would like to have a wife."

8 Discuss the following questions.

a What makes the text ironic?

b Why has the author decided to write about a wife and not about a husband?

c Are wives like the one described in the text common in your community? Why (not)?

d Look at the illustration below. In your opinion, how is the message of the illustration related to the message of the text on the previous page?

IMAGE COURTESY ANNE TAINTOR, INC.

Genre Analysis

1 Choose the three correct endings to characterize a call for participation.

A call for participation:

a ☐ is usually a formal questionnaire.

b ☐ contains an invitation.

c ☐ usually describes an event.

d ☐ offers a way to register for an event.

e ☐ is written in the first person singular.

f ☐ is directed to a particular audience.

g ☐ can be published or broadcast.

2 The text on page 51 is divided in three parts. Using your answers to activity 1 above, write the main characteristic of each part.

a Learn (part 1)

b Share (part 2)

c Act (part 3)

3 Read the call for proposals below and add a fourth characteristic to the ones listed in activity 2.

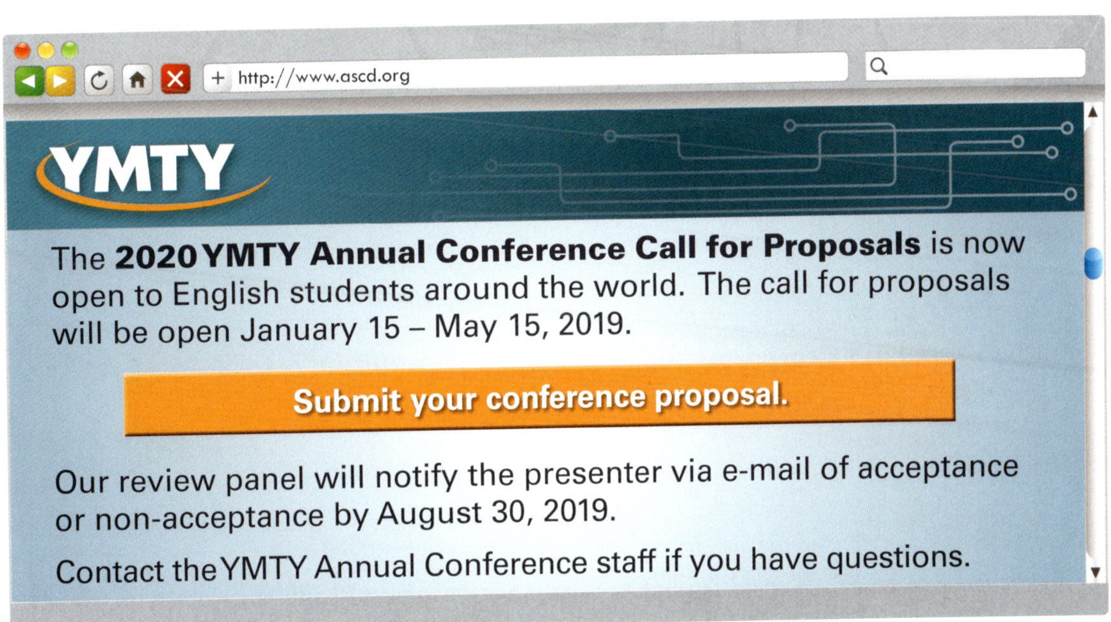

RAFAEL GENTILE

Based on <www.ascd.org>. Accessed on Oct 30, 2012.

Vocabulary

1 Write the missing months in the 2019 calendar. Use a dictionary if necessary.

RAFAEL GENTILE

2 In English we use ordinal numbers to say dates. Complete the chart below.

1st	first	11th	eleventh
2nd	second	12th	twelfth
3rd	third	13th	
4th	fourth	15th	
5th	fifth	20th	twentieth
6th		21st	twenty-first
7th		22nd	
8th	eighth	23rd	
9th	ninth	30th	
10th	tenth	31st	

Did you know

There are two systems to write the dates in digits:
In American English the order is month, day, and year: 4/26/1961.
In British English the order is day, month, and year: 26/4/1961.

3 Write the dates mentioned in the sentences below.

a On **July 20, 1969**, Neil Armstrong and Buzz Aldrin landed on the moon.

____

b Brazil declared its independence from Portugal on **September 7, 1822**.

____

c The Kyoto Protocol was first adopted on **11 December, 1997**.

____

d Terrorists attacked the World Trade Center on **September 11, 2001**.

____

4 Choose the best definition for the highlighted words and expressions.

- In 2000 our leaders decided to **halve**[1] extreme poverty by 2015.
- Inequality is **growing**[2] and our planet is at risk.
- **Join**[3] the Global Conversation! Contribute to **shaping**[4] the post-2015 development agenda.
- This is an opportunity to discuss the **issues**[5] we **care about**[6] most. We can build a **sustainable**[7] future by the people and for the people.

a [1] reduce something to half its original number or size

b [ ] expanding

c [ ] become a participant

d [ ] problems

e [ ] be interested in because we consider important

f [ ] giving form to something

g [ ] able to be maintained / continued

5 Match the icons to the words / expressions they represent.

a governance

b inequalities

c growth and employment

d health

e education

f environmental sustainability

g food security and nutrition

h conflict and fragility

i population dynamics

j energy

k water

RAFAEL GENTILE/ROBERTA BENITES

Grammar

1 In the call for participation on page 51, the words *learn*, *share*, and *act* are examples of:

a ☐ adjectives. **b** ☐ nouns. **c** ☐ verbs.

2 These three words are used in the text to:

a ☐ say actions in progress at the moment we speak.

b ☐ give commands, instructions, or suggestions.

c ☐ talk about past events with a defined time.

3 The communicative intention of these words in the text is expressed by:

a ☐ the Simple Present. **b** ☐ the imperative form. **c** ☐ the auxiliary verb.

4 To make the *World We Want*, we need some practical steps for action. Choose one of the topics (see previous page) and write your suggestions.

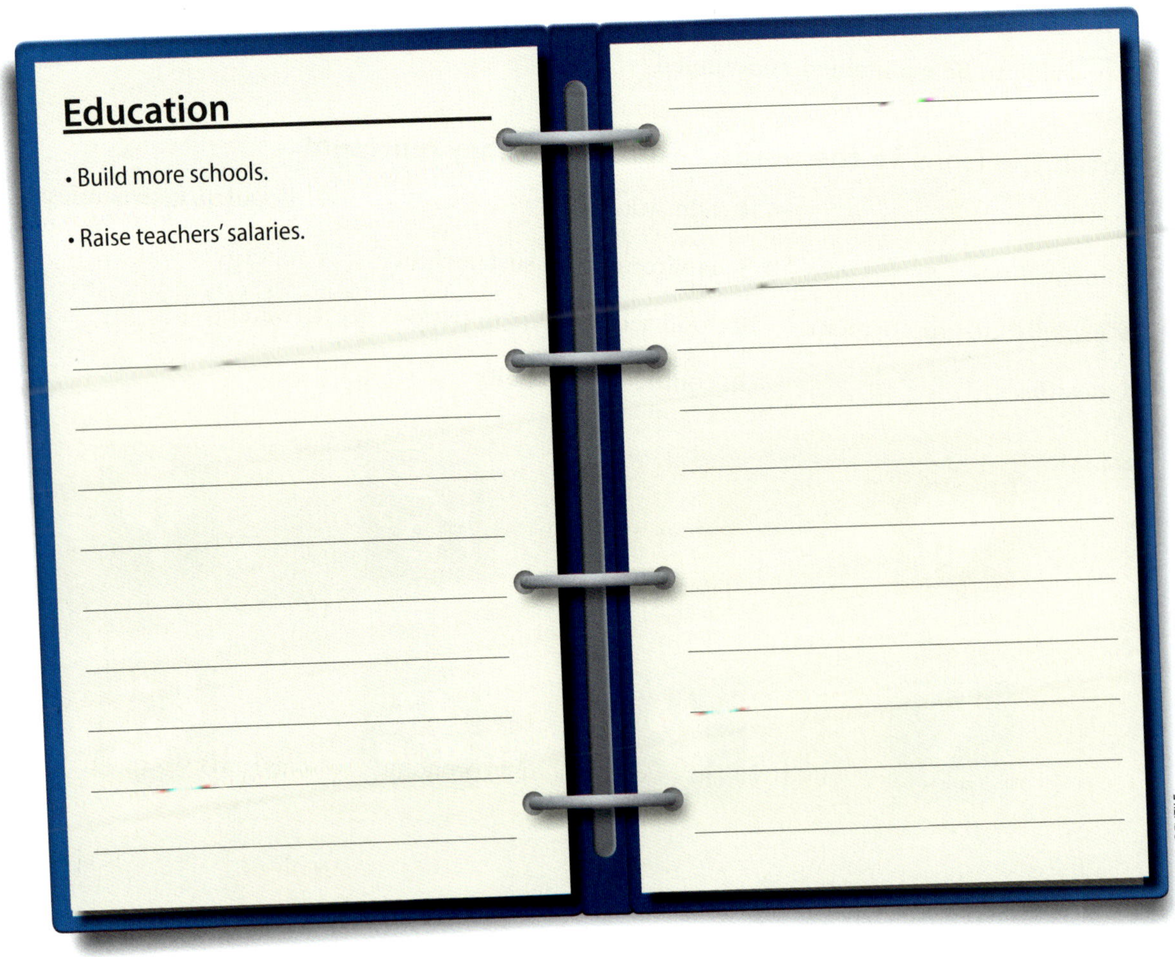

RAFAEL GENTILE

In Other Words

Imperativo

A forma imperativa dos verbos geralmente é utilizada para expressar instruções, ordens ou sugestões.

1

Instrução:
Mix all the ingredients.

Ordem: Stay!

3

2

Sugestão:
Don't lift too much weight.

ART: SELECT; PHOTOS: JUPITERIMAGES/CREATAS RF/THINKSTOCK (1); BRAND X/THINKSTOCK, JUPITERIMAGES/CREATAS RF/THINKSTOCK (2); ANDY DEAN/ISTOCKPHOTO/THINKSTOCK (3)

Em inglês, para formar o imperativo afirmativo, usa-se o verbo na forma infinitiva (ou seja, sem conjugá-lo) e sem *to:*

to learn → **learn**
to share → **share**
to act → **act**

Para formar o imperativo negativo, coloca-se *do not* / *don't* antes do verbo:

Do not throw food away.
Don't waste water.

Com verbos na forma imperativa, não é necessário usar pronomes pessoais, uma vez que o pronome "você(s)" (*you*) está implícito.

Para fazer pedidos ou solicitações, acrescenta-se a palavra *please* no final ou no início da oração:

Pick up your trash, **please**.
Please, reduce your waste.

Practice Makes Perfect

1 Read the text about how to be a sustainable and respectful tourist and complete it with the verbs below. Use the imperative form in the affirmative or negative.

ask buy choose dress eat
enter learn talk touch use

sustainable /səˈsteɪnəb(ə)l/ adjective using methods that do not harm the environment

Do's and Don'ts While Traveling

Your Travel Choice Makes a Difference

By exploring alternative travel choices, you can have a unique trip and avoid leaving negative marks on cultures, economies, and the environment.

1. At the hotel: Ask about environmental laws and practices. ________ with the locals about working conditions.

2. Language: ________ a few words of the local language and use them.

3. Clothes: ________ inappropriately; read about local conventions before you go. In many countries, modest dress is important.

4. Behavior: Be respectful of local citizens' privacy. ________ sacred places, homes, or private places before asking permission.

5. Photos: Be sensitive to when and where you take photos or make a video of people. Always ________ first.

6. Environment: Respect the natural environment. ________ or disturb animals. Always follow designated trails.

7. Animal products: ________ products made from protected or endangered animals.

8. Buy local: ________ hotels that belong to local people. ________ local buses, car rental agencies, and airlines. ________ in local restaurants, shop in local markets, and attend local festivals / events.

RAFAEL GENTILE/ROBERTA BENITES

Adapted from <www.ecotourism.org>. Accessed on Jan 10, 2013.

2 What would you say or suggest to the people in the situations below? Follow the example.

a A man is talking on his cell phone during the movie. Make a request.

You: *Turn off your phone, please.*

b Your friend wants to lose weight.

You: ________

c A new student in school doesn't know how to get to the restroom. Give him / her instructions.

You: ________

d Your classmate is speaking Portuguese in an English oral exam. Make a request.

You: ________

The Way It Sounds

1 Look at the map and answer the questions below.

a What continent is it?

____

b What country is zoomed in?

____

c What do you know about this country?

____

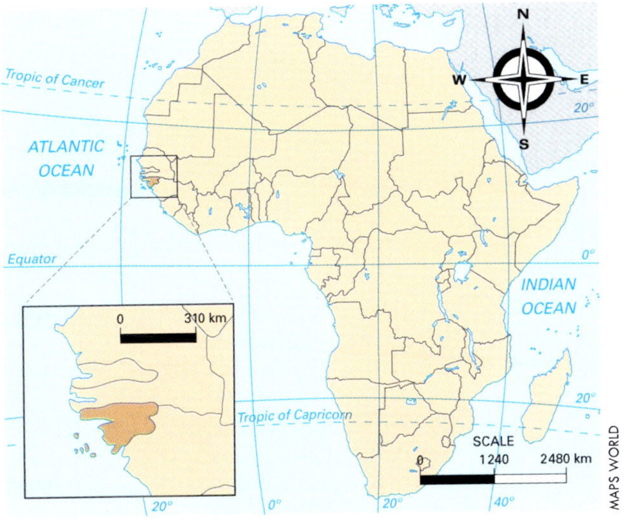

Based on *Atlas geográfico escolar*. Rio de Janeiro: IBGE, 2009. p. 45.

2 Listen to the first part of a story told by a volunteer working with children's education in Guinea-Bissau. Cross out the incorrect alternative in each sentence.

6

a The story is about a **10 year-old girl** / **10 girls from a city** called Anita.

b The girl **goes to school** / **does her chores** early in the morning.

c There are 18 **rooms** / **people** in the girl's house.

d Her **home** / **school** is made of mud bricks and covered with a metal roof.

e Guinea-Bissau is one of the **poorest** / **richest** countries in the world.

f The girl lives in a place where **there is** / **there is no** running water and electricity.

3 Listen to the second part of the story and answer the questions.

7

a What does Anita have to do to get water every morning?

____

b How long did she have to walk before the new well was built?

____

c Why is this new well important for Anita's studies?

____

d What does Anita want to do in the future?

____

4 In your opinion, is there any way to help children like Anita to change their lives? How? Discuss with a partner.

TalkActive

Discuss the changes you can make in your community.

Preparation

- Match some expressions used in opinion discussions with their meanings. The first one is done for you.

~~ask for an opinion~~ | explain / correct something | express agreement | express disagreement | make interruptions | give an opinion

a *What do you think? Do you agree?* are used to ask for an opinion.

b *I think... In my opinion... I feel...* are used to ______

c *I agree (with you). You're right. That's true! Exactly!* are used to ______

d *I (totally) disagree. I don't think so.* are used to ______

e *I mean...* is used to ______

f *Sorry to interrupt, but... May I say something?* are used to ______

- Check the alternatives that define an opinion discussion.

a ☐ It involves two or more people.

b ☐ It is usually about a topic considered important by the people involved.

c ☐ It is always finished when everybody agrees on a solution.

d ☐ It sometimes involves giving information about the topic.

e ☐ It involves sharing different opinions on the topic.

f ☐ It involves a detailed research about the topic.

The discussion

- Choose one topic below.
  - What can you do to reduce the use of water and energy in your community?
  - What can you do to help your community treat men and women equally?
  - What kind of volunteer work can you do to help make our world better?
- Discuss the topic you chose with your group.

Sharing

- Share your conclusions with another group.
  - What can you all do to take action and change your community?
- Choose the best suggestions in your groups and share them with your class.

Self-assessment

MAURO SOUZA

AO FINAL DESTA UNIDADE, JÁ SOU CAPAZ DE	
identificar os objetivos, os meios de veiculação, as características e o público-alvo de *calls for participation*.	
ler e refletir sobre a desigualdade no posicionamento de mulheres e homens.	
compreender e usar diferentes formas de se referir a datas.	
reconhecer o emprego e a função comunicativa da forma imperativa dos verbos.	
discutir sobre as contribuições pessoais para a melhoria das condições de vida no planeta.	

Se você deixou de marcar algum dos itens na tabela de autoavaliação, procure no *site* deste livro atividades extras que o ajudem a praticar e consolidar os tópicos desta unidade.

Going Beyond

Websites

- A report on the progress in achieving the Millennium Development Goals: <www.un.org/en/development/desa/publications/mdg-report-2012.html>.
- The lyrics and video of the song "We are the world", by Michael Jackson and Lionel Richie, made for the group USA for Africa: <www.youtube.com/watch?v=ne7fPpxAnuM>.

3

Objeto educacional digital

JOHN STANMEYER/VII/CORBIS/LATINSTOCK

HOW CAN YOU CHANGE THE WORLD?

NESTA UNIDADE VOCÊ IRÁ:

- identificar as características de um *feature article*;
- escrever um *informative flyer*;
- usar pronomes pessoais e oblíquos;
- fazer uma apresentação oral sobre problemas enfrentados em sua comunidade e ações para lidar com eles.

ROBERTO SCHMIDT/AFP/GETTY IMAGES

unit 4

SASCHA BURKARD/ISTOCKPHOTO/THINKSTOCK

- Que problemas são mostrados nas fotografias? Eles são comuns na região onde você mora?
- Que problemas futuros você imagina que poderão acontecer em decorrência dessas situações?

Have Your Say

Human Sciences

1 The Human Development Index (HDI) is a way to measure human development in every country and society. It is calculated by the United Nations Development Program (UNDP), an organization that focuses on fighting poverty in the world. These three dimensions are considered in the HDI. Put them in the correct place.

education | GNI per capita | life expectancy at birth

The length of time that someone will possibly live: ____________________

The process of providing people with information: ____________________

The total money earned or gained by the people who live in a country over a period of time: ____________________

2 Analyze the HDI map below and answer: Are you surprised with Brazil's result? Why (not)?

____

____

HDI: Human Development Index (HDI) value (2011)

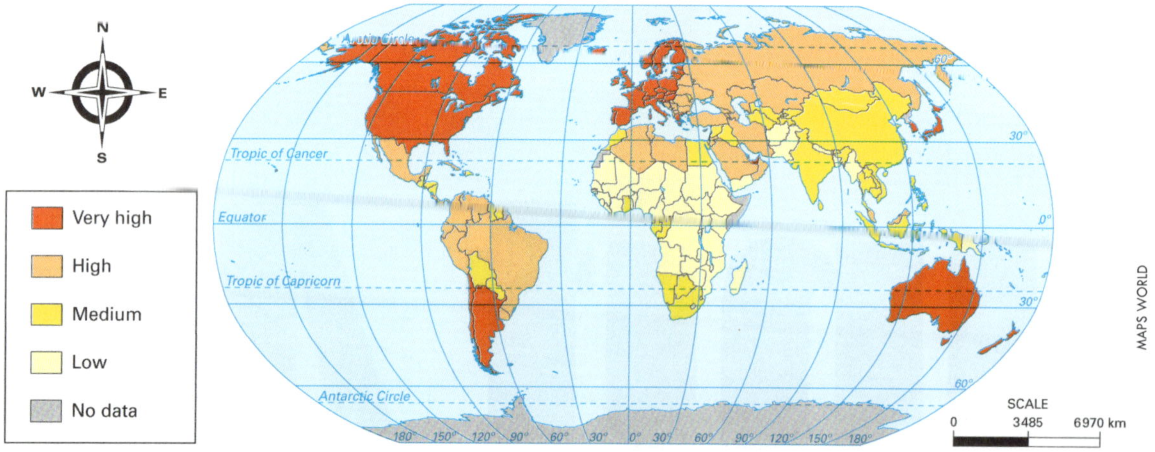

Based on <http://hdr.undp.org>. Accessed on March 4, 2013.

3 Research the current HDI results for your city. What is its current position in the ranking? What can you do to make a difference and improve the position of your city?

TIP

Stay informed about the HDI in your community. This is important because with more information we can help to find solutions to the problems and ask our government for results.

4 Read the quote below by Paulo Freire, a Brazilian educator internationally respected for his work, and answer the questions.

> *"Once present in the world, it is impossible not to contribute to the creation of this world."*
>
> (Paulo Freire, 2000)

a Do you agree with Paulo Freire? Why (not)?

____

b Do you think you contribute to the creation of the world you live in? If yes, how?

____

c Does school provide you with opportunities to learn how you can contribute to changing the world? How?

____

____

5 Read the statements below and choose a sentence to express your opinion about them.

I agree/disagree. | I strongly agree/disagree. | I don't know/ have an opinion.

a Everybody can do something to change the world. ______________

b You can only help change the world if you are very rich. ______________

c Changing the world depends on how old you are. ______________

d You can learn many ways to help change the world at school. ______________

6 Justify your opinion to your classmates. Do you all agree?

7 Read the statements below and circle if they are true (T) or false (F) about you.

a I treat other people the way I want to be treated.	T	F
b I don't intentionally ridicule, embarrass, or hurt other people.	T	F
c I try to have creative solutions for the problems I face.	T	F
d I try to help people when they have a problem or need something.	T	F
e I do things in order to benefit all the people involved, not only myself.	T	F

8 Discuss your answers with a classmate. Tell each other why you behave the way you do. Is there any behavior that you think you should change? Why (not)?

Reading Beyond the Words

1 Read this introduction to a feature article and choose the correct alternative to complete the statements.

http://mom.me/
mom.me
Teens Who Are Changing the World
These kids are already making a huge difference
A Source of Inspiration
by JENNA BIRCH

A 15-year-old finding a better way to detect one of the deadliest forms of cancer? A young girl challenging the distorted perception of beauty in the fashion industry? A 19-year-old who might help rocket scientists get probes to deep space? Meet the young people who are putting us to shame, changing industries – and ultimately changing the world.

NEXT

1 2 3 4 5 6

Extracted from <http://mom.me/>. Accessed on Dec 22, 2012.

a The aim of the introduction above is to:

☐ introduce some teens and their ideas. ☐ present some world problems and solutions.

b The teens are in the news because they:

☐ can solve industrial problems. ☐ have ideas to change the world.

c The problems mentioned are related to:

☐ health and natural resources. ☐ age and changing space.

d The feature article was written by ___________ and published on a ___________

☐ genius kids / in a teens magazine. ☐ Jenna Birch / on a website.

2 Choose one of the two texts on the next page to read and answer the questions.

a What's his / her name and how old is he / she?

____

b What's the problem he / she is worried about?

____

c Why is each problem they deal with important to adults and teens alike?

____

d What are his / her ideas to solve the problem? Highlight them in the feature article you read.

____

http://mom.me/

mom.me

Teens Who Are Changing the World

PREV 5 of 14 NEXT

These kids are already making a huge difference

1

Jack Andraka, 15

Pancreatic cancer is one of the most dangerous forms of cancer there is. In five years, 94 percent of those with the disease die. Finally, there's a better and cheaper way to diagnose it more quickly. The test, created by 15-year-old Jack Andraka, detects an abnormal protein that indicates the disease. "I got interested in early detection, because that's the best chance of treating cancer," he said, according to TIME. "The only practical way of doing this is doing routine blood tests, so that's my idea." For this innovation, he received first prize in the Intel International Science and Engineering Fair and $100,000. Smart kid that he is, he's saving the money for college.

2

Julia Bluhm, 14

Julia Bluhm wasn't happy with the way the young fashion magazines portray beauty, so she petitioned to change the face of the industry, asking *Seventeen* to stop retouching photos in their pages – and got 84,000 signatures in agreement. Her plea to editor Ann Shocket read, "Here's what lots of girls don't know. Those 'pretty women' that we see in magazines are... often photoshopped, airbrushed, edited to look thinner... I've learned that we have the power to fight back." Shocket listened to her. She made the entire *Seventeen* staff sign a Body Peace Treaty never to alter a model's face or body. Other young teens of an activist group named Spark recently visited *Teen Vogue*'s offices with a similar plea, but they were ignored by the publication.

Adapted from <http://mom.me/>. Accessed on Dec 22, 2012.

3 Tell your partner what you know about Jack or Julia. Then, check the correct answers below.

a From the title Teens Who Are Changing the World we can infer that these teens inspire us to:

- ☐ give ideas about life improvement for free with no financial return.
- ☐ create or do something that can improve people's lives on our planet.
- ☐ work hard to find solutions for health problems and to create tech innovations.

b The author of the feature article believes that:

- ☐ smart teenagers can work to change the world.
- ☐ teenagers are unaware of the world's problems.
- ☐ only teenagers have brilliant ideas for innovations.

4 List two people who have made a difference in your city and explain your choices to a classmate. How are they similar to / different from Julia and Jack?

Genre Analysis

1 Feature articles are published in magazines, newspapers, and on different sites on the Internet. They focus on general subjects that interest the audience they are written for.

Which are some of the general characteristics of feature articles? Check them below.

- ☐ Feature articles are not usually outdated after months or years of publication.
- ☐ They focus on people, provide their profiles and quotes from them, for example.
- ☐ They have attractive titles to provoke readers' interest and motivate them to read.
- ☐ They are neutral pieces of news, and the writer's opinion is never given.

2 Identify the elements of a feature article in the text below.

a **author's identification**

b **catchy title** – one that provokes readers' interest and enhances their motivation.

c **headline** – a phrase at the top of an article indicating the subject of the article, usually in a large font size.

d **introduction to the feature article**

e **lead** – a phrase used to add information to the headline.

☐ Teens Who Are Changing the World

☐ These kids are already making a huge difference

☐ by JENNA BIRCH

☐ A Source of Inspiration

☐ A 15-year-old finding a better way to detect one of the deadliest forms of cancer? A young girl challenging the distorted perception of beauty in the fashion industry? A 19-year-old who might help rocket scientists get probes to deep space? Meet the young people who are putting us to shame, changing industries – and ultimately changing the world. NEXT

Vocabulary

1 Use the health-related words / expressions below to complete the sentences.

blood test | diagnosed | dies | disease | to treat

a I have a ______________ once a year during my medical checkup.

b Do you know how ______________ a headache without medicine?

c My cousin was ______________ with food allergies. There are many things he cannot eat.

d According to the American Cancer Society, one person ______________ of melanoma every 57 minutes.

e Diabetes is a ______________ in which the body produces too little insulin or does not use insulin properly, or both.

2 Underline two synonyms for the words in bold.

a Meet the young people who are putting us to **shame**, changing industries – and ultimately changing the world.

discredit | humiliation | respect

b Julia Bluhm wasn't happy with the way the young fashion magazines **portray** beauty.

distort | illustrate | represent

c She **petitioned** to change the face of the industry, asking *Seventeen* to stop **retouching** photos in their pages.

demanded | refused | requested
improving | repairing | worsening

d Her **plea** to editor Ann Shocket read, "Here's what lots of girls don't know. Those 'pretty women' that we see in magazines are… often photoshopped, airbrushed, edited to look thinner."

alibi | argument | justification

e Shocket listened to her. She made the entire *Seventeen* **staff** sign a Body Peace **Treaty** never to alter a model's face or body.

readers | team | workers
convention | disagreement | pact

Grammar

1 **Below you will find some sentences from the texts about Jack Andraka and Julia Bluhm. Circle the subject pronouns and underline the object pronouns.**

"I got interested in early detection, because that's the best chance of treating cancer."

"Finally, there's a better and cheaper way to diagnose it more quickly."

"I've learned that we have the power to fight back."

"Shocket listened to her. She made the entire *Seventeen* staff sign a Body Peace Treaty."

ERIKA ONODERA

2 **Find the sentences above in the texts on page 69, and choose from the words below what / whom the underlined pronouns refer to.**

Jack Andraka — Julia Bluhm — pancreatic cancer — teenagers

a "I got interested in early detection…" *I* refers to ____________________.

b "… there's a better and cheaper way to diagnose it more quickly." *It* refers to ____________________.

c "… we have the power to fight back." *We* refers to ____________________.

d "Shocket listened to her…" *Her* refers to ____________________.

3 **Complete the table below.**

Subject pronouns	Object pronouns
	me
you	you
	him
she	her
	it
	us
you	
they	

In Other Words

Pronomes pessoais

Os pronomes pessoais são as palavras que substituem os nomes, indicando diretamente as pessoas do discurso.

Eles podem assumir a função de sujeito ou predicativo do sujeito (caso reto) ou a função de complemento (caso oblíquo).

Em inglês, há a seguinte classificação gramatical dos pronomes:

✔ *Subject pronouns* – correspondem ao sujeito da oração, aquele que executa determinada ação ou que se encontra em determinado estado.

Subject pronouns	Sujeito da oração (aquele que executa uma ação)
I	**I** am interested in a cure for cancer.
you	**You** can help change the world.
he	**He** is a very famous Brazilian educator.
she	**She** works for *Seventeen Magazine*.
it	**It** is our responsibility to save our planet.
we	**We** teach people music and art.
you	**You** are all creative teens.
they	**They** help people solve their problems.

✔ *Object pronouns* – correspondem ao objeto do verbo, aquele que recebe a ação.

Object pronouns	Objeto do verbo (aquele que recebe a ação)
me	I don't understand. Can you help **me**?
you	Carla is looking for **you**.
him	Vicente is a nice guy; let's invite **him** to the party.
her	Editor Ann Shocket talked to **her** about the article.
it	The world needs help. You can change **it**.
us	The volunteers helped **us** after the hurricane.
you	Ann and Phil, this gift is for **you**.
them	People in Haiti need food; let's help **them**.

Practice Makes Perfect

1 Circle the pronoun that completes each sentence correctly.

a I need to see the doctor. I'll call **she / her** to make an appointment.

b Pancreatic cancer is the 4th overall cause of cancer-related deaths in the U.S. because **it / he** is relatively symptom-free in the early stages.

c My grandfather has always believed that a strict diet and daily exercise help avoid diseases. It seems to work for **he / him**. **He / Him** is 80 and healthy.

d Jack Andraka created a test to diagnose pancreatic cancer more quickly. **It / He** detects an abnormal protein that's an indicator of the disease.

e Mackenzie Bearup asks around for used books. Then **her / she** donates **they / them** to people in need.

2 Complete the conversation with the correct subject or object pronoun.

Sandra: I read about a girl named Julia Bluhm. ________ asked a teen magazine to stop photoshopping the models.

Paul: Why?

Sandra: ________ says ________ are not a real representation of women.

Paul: And do ________ agree with ________?

Sandra: Yes, ________ do. The photographs make ________ believe ________ are fat and ugly when we are not. Does it happen in male magazines too?

Paul: Sure, ________ does. ________ show a very unrealistic image of men. I never buy ________.

ART: RAFAEL GENTILE / PHOTO: JOSHUA HODGE PHOTOGRAPHY/ ISTOCKPHOTO/THINKSTOCK

3 Rewrite the paragraph below using pronouns in the place of the underlined words to avoid repetition.

Jack and Liz are old friends; Jack and Liz met in elementary school many years ago. Jack is in love with Liz, so Jack wants to propose to Liz. Liz likes Jack as a friend, but Liz doesn't think of Jack as a boyfriend. We know that, if Liz says "no" to Jack, Jack will be devastated. But Jack did not ask Mary and me what our opinion was, so there is nothing Mary and I can do to help.

SELECT

4 Use the verbs below and pronouns to express how you feel about the people and things listed.

hate | like / not like | love | not care about

1

Soccer

I hate it. / I like it. / I don't like them. / I love it. / I don't care about them.

2

Adele

____

6

Robert Pattinson

____

3

Comic books

____

7

Coffee

____

4

Marcelo Adnet

____

8

Paula Fernandes

____

5

Chocolate

____

9

Word puzzles

____

ART: SELECT; PHOTOS: PIXLAND/THINKSTOCK (1); FEATURE FLASH/DREAMSTIME.COM (2); MIETITORE/DREAMSTIME.COM (3); FÁBIO GUINALZ/FOTOARENA (4); SUTI/DREAMSTIME.COM (5); FEATURE FLASH/DREAMSTIME.COM (6); STOCKSNAPPER/ISTOCKPHOTO/THINKSTOCK (7); FÁBIO GUINALZ/FOTOARENA (8); PRESCOTT09/DREAMSTIME.COM (9)

Put It in Writing

Plan your writing.

What to write: An informative flyer.

Purpose: To call people's attention to a specific problem in your neighborhood.

Audience: The community where you live.

Brainstorm some of the problems you face in your neighborhood and choose one. Make a chart in your notebook to write your notes. Look at the example below.

Problem	Reasons	Action
trash on the streets	it causes floods it's not good for our health	use trash bins

Study the flyer made for the example given above. Complete with the information from the chart.

ART: RAFAEL GENTILE/ROBERTA BENITES; PHOTO: COMSTOCK IMAGES/THINKSTOCK

Flyers are announcements or advertisement printed on a piece of paper and distributed to people or posted in public places.

Major characteristics:

- interesting and attractive layout;
- use of images, charts, or illustrations;
- effective position of the information to facilitate reading;
- text is short, direct, and concise.

Design and write your flyer. Remember to use images and titles. Make it attractive and interesting. Use the checklist below to revise your text.

	Yes	No
1 It respects the characteristics of the genre.		
2 It meets my writing objectives.		
3 The language is appropriate to my audience.		
4 The text uses good grammar and punctuation.		

- If you checked *no* in any topic above, rewrite your flyer.

Publish your flyer.

The Way It Sounds

1 Discuss the questions and justify your answers.

a What do you know about space exploration?

b Would you like to be able to explore the universe?

interviewer /ˈɪntərˌvjuər/ noun [C] someone who interviews people, especially as a job

interviewee /ˌɪntərvjuˈi/ noun [C] someone who is being interviewed

NASA, ESA, AND THE HUBBLE HERITAGE TEAM (STSCI/AURA)

Galaxy Messier 82 (M82)

2 Listen to an interview with a teen who is changing the world. Check the correct alternative to complete the statements about it.

8

a There are ____________ people talking. ☐ two ☐ three

b They are an interviewer and a ____________. ☐ scientist ☐ teen

c The interviewee is a ____________. ☐ girl ☐ boy

d The interviewee's name is ____________. ☐ Aisha Mustafa ☐ Alison Mustang

3 Listen to the interview again and complete the sentences.

9

a Aisha is from ____________.

b She is ____________ years old.

c She is worried about the ____________ of fuel.

d It is important because the cost of fuel limits ____________ exploration.

e Her idea to solve the problem is to use little ____________ from space for propulsion.

f If Aisha can prove her theory, everything we know about the ____________ can change.

4 Discuss your answers to the questions below.

a How can a teenager, who's not a qualified professional, develop a theory about space particles?

b Where can people learn things to develop theories like Aisha's?

c What do people need in order to be able to make proposals to change the world?

TalkActive

Prepare a picture-based oral presentation to show social problems faced by your community.

> **caption** /ˈkæpʃ(ə)n/ noun [C] words printed near or on a picture that explain something about the picture

Preparation

- Check what is true about the genre "picture-based slide."

  ☐ Picture-based slides focus on illustrations, accompanied by short captions.
  ☐ These types of slides are usually created for oral presentations.
  ☐ They contain long pieces of written information to guide the presentation.
  ☐ The captions are written in an adequate font size so they can be read at a distance.

- From the list below, choose four or five of the most severe problems faced by your community. Add others if you want. Think about what you can do to help.

Poverty
- ☐ homeless people living on the streets
- ☐ adult beggars everywhere
- ☐ children asking for money at traffic lights
- ☐ ____________________

Pollution
- ☐ air polluted by smoke from factories and cars
- ☐ polluted water of lakes and rivers
- ☐ stinky smell from open sewers
- ☐ ____________________

Education
- ☐ inadequate public transportation to schools
- ☐ lack of magazines for teens and comic books in English in the school library
- ☐ not enough English classes per week
- ☐ ____________________

Citizenship
- ☐ lack of public campaigns for educating people to become better citizens
- ☐ deaths caused by irresponsible drivers
- ☐ trash spread in the streets, on the roads, and in the school's backyard
- ☐ ____________________

CAROL DURAN

- Select pictures that illustrate the problems faced by your community. Take on-site pictures around your town / city. Show all the pictures to your English teacher to check if they are appropriate for your set of slides.
- Create your set of slides (maximum of 6). Give it a catchy title. Add a lead if you want. Place each picture on one slide. Write a short caption for each of them.
- Revise your work. Check below.

Do your slides look attractive?	☐ Yes	☐ No
Are the slides cluttered with too much information?	☐ Yes	☐ No
Are the captions short and informative?	☐ Yes	☐ No

The presentation

- Keep eye contact with your audience.
- Speak as naturally as you can.
- Keep track of time!
- Be well prepared to answer your classmates' questions.

Self-assessment

MAURO SOUZA

AO FINAL DESTA UNIDADE, JÁ SOU CAPAZ DE	
identificar as características e a intenção comunicativa de *feature articles*.	
reconhecer o emprego e a função comunicativa de pronomes.	
elaborar orações usando pronomes pessoais do caso reto e do caso oblíquo.	
fazer uma apresentação oral sobre problemas enfrentados em minha comunidade e possíveis ações para lidar com eles.	
escrever um *informative flyer*.	

Se você deixou de marcar algum dos itens na tabela de autoavaliação, procure no *site* deste livro atividades extras que o ajudem a praticar e consolidar os tópicos desta unidade.

Going Beyond

Song

- "Heal the world". Michael Jackson. Its lyrics speak of creating a better world, especially for future generations. The music video shows children living in violent societies.

Movie

- *Quem se importa*. 2012. Documentary. This movie looks into the initiatives of 19 entrepreneurs in the area of social work – among them the Nobel laureate Muhammad Yunus.

4

Objeto educacional digital

Nurse

What is it like to be a nurse? Read the online article below.

www.whyzz.com

home | about | answer | mobile | newsletter | blog

What does a nurse do? by Mya Kagan

Nurses work in lots of different places like hospitals, doctor's offices, clinics, people's homes, schools, camps, and more! Depending on where they work and the level of training they've had, nurses can do a big variety of different things. Some nurses take temperatures, give shots, administer medicines, and check patients' blood pressure and pulse. Other nurses may prescribe medications, order tests, and help diagnose a patient's problem. There are nurses who assist doctors during surgery and nurses who help deliver babies!

Lots of nurses work closely with patients and families, helping them, supporting them, and educating them about things they need to know to take care of their illnesses and stay healthy and happy.

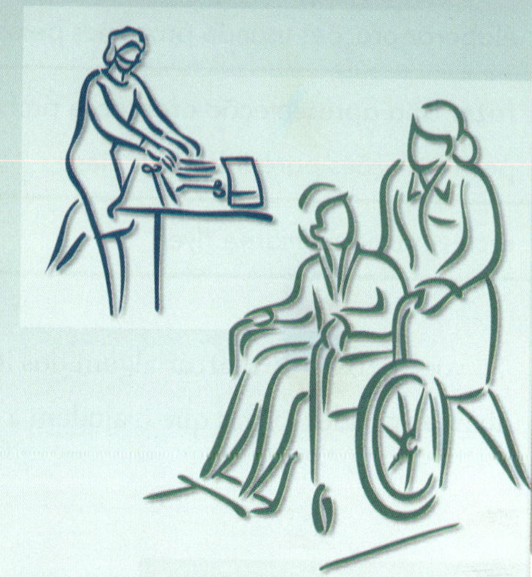

RAFAEL GENTILE

Adapted from <www.whyzz.com>. Accessed on Nov 9, 2012.

Do you have the key skills to become a nurse? Check YES or NO in the table below.

Are you good at:	Yes	No
helping and caring for others?		
paying attention to what other people are saying?		
concentrating on a task without being distracted?		
telling when something is wrong?		
documenting and recording information?		
making decisions under pressure?		
using scientific rules and methods?		

Would you like to be a nurse? Why?

FACT FILES (part II)

Read the fact file about volunteering experience and fill in the boxes below with the corresponding number.

VOLUNTEERING EXPERIENCE

JUPITERIMAGES/CREATAS RF/THINKSTOCK

Benefits	• **Providing**[1] new skills. • Gaining real-life experience. • Exploring **career fields**[2]. • Making connections (networking). • Increasing self-confidence. • Getting personal satisfaction.
Skills developed in volunteer work	• Leadership experience by creating a program, leading other people, organizing an event, etc. • People skills **by working**[3] with others, teaming up with other volunteers or with individuals, developing sensitivity to the needs and feelings of others. • Personality by being productive and assertive, working well with others. • Group-mindedness by working as a team to meet goals.
Volunteer requirements	• Anyone can become a great volunteer as everybody has talents and skills. • Opportunities for every age, but most volunteer programs **are**[4] for people age 16 and older.

Adapted from <www.illinoisworknet.com>. Accessed on Nov 9, 2012.

[ ] use of the Present Simple

[1] use of *-ing* forms for items in lists of activities

[ ] use of *-ing* forms after prepositions

[ ] word order: adjectives + nouns

SELF-STUDY units 3 - 4

1. As you discussed in units 3 and 4, we have to be committed to protecting the world we live in. Read the poster below, which calls people to take action for a better environment, and check the incorrect statements.

SERGIO ONODERA

- [ ] Students can register on the morning of the event.
- [ ] All students who register get a T shirt.
- [ ] Only students from class 301 can participate in the beach cleaning competition.
- [ ] If people need information, there's a phone number they should call.
- [ ] Students have to take their own water bottles and sunscreen.

2. Read the announcement below and use the information from the poster above to make it complete and meaningful.

__________ 301 is proud to announce the *2015 Beach Cleaning Morning*! Participants will meet by the Duke Kahanamoku Statue, on Waikiki Beach, and students in grades __________ can join us. Register until March 14th and your __________ is guaranteed. And last but not least, use __________ and bring your __________ bottle along. See you then!

Duke Kahanamoku Statue on Waikiki Beach.

AURORA OPEN/GETTY IMAGES

3. **Which instructions would you use in the following social situations? Refer back to pages 58 and 59 to review the use of these instructions.**

cross (neg) | eat | forget (neg) | close | skip (neg) | turn down

a The light is red. — You: _______________ the street, Amanda!

b You want to sleep and your brother is listening to music. — You: _______________ the radio, please.

c It's very cold outside and your classmate opens the window. — You: Hey, _______________ the window, please! It's cold!

d You need to remind your mom to buy you a new Spanish dictionary. — You: Mom, _______________ to buy me a new Spanish dictionary.

e Dad needs to balance his eating habits, but he doesn't know how. — You: _______________ every three hours and _______________ meals, daddy.

4. **There are so many things each one of us can do to help save our planet. Read the tips below to find out what. Then underline the verbs in the imperative.**

1 Replace your regular light bulbs with compact fluorescent bulbs. Don't like the color of the light? Use these bulbs for closets, laundry rooms, and other places where it won't annoy you as much.

2 Turn off computers at night. If you don't want to wait for your computer to start up, set it to turn on automatically a few minutes before you get to work.

3 Don't rinse dishes before using your dishwasher.

4 Don't pre-heat the oven. Just turn it on when you put the dish in.

5 Recycle glass. If it isn't recycled, it can take a million years to decompose.

6 Hang dry: get a clothesline or rack to dry your clothes by air.

7 Go vegetarian once a week. One less meat-based meal a week helps the planet and your diet.

8 Ban bath time! Have a no-bath week, and take showers instead.

9 Use both sides of paper. And when you're finished with your documents, don't forget to take them to the recycling bin.

10 Turn off lights: Always turn off incandescent bulbs when you leave a room. Fluorescent bulbs are more affected by the number of times they are switched on and off, so turn them off when you leave a room for 15 minutes or more.

Adapted from <www.50waystohelp.com>. Accessed on Nov 12, 2012.

annoy (verb): incomodar
dishwasher (noun): lava-louça
instead (adv.): em vez disso
pre-heat (verb): pré-aquecer

5. **Go back to pages 72, 73, and 74. Review subject and object pronouns and when they are used. Then rewrite the sentences replacing the underlined words with subject or object pronouns.**

a I love Catherine.
I love her_______________________________________.

b Sorry, Mr. Schuester, my friends and I are late.
_______________________________________.

c Thomas brought his sneakers today.
_______________________________________.

d Sing with Terry and me.
_______________________________________.

e Clarissa was by the door.
_______________________________________.

f I don't like the new technologies.
_______________________________________.

g Who was talking to you and Sarah?
_______________________________________?

6. **Take a look at the short conversations that follow. They all need to be completed in order to deliver meaningful messages. Fill in the blanks with the correct use of subject and object pronouns.**

a Liam: Susie, where is Aunt Fernanda?
Susie: __________ think __________'s at the university. Do __________ need to talk to__________?
Liam: Yeah, I need a ride to our friends' house. __________ are going to start our project today.

☐ you – she – I – him – we ☐ I – she – you – she – we ☐ I – she – you – her – we

b Ted is a good friend, but __________ never returns the things he borrows. From now on I won't lend __________ anything. __________ love my books and I want to take good care of __________.

☐ him – he – I – them ☐ he – him – I – them ☐ he – him – he – it

c Paula: Who are those guys? I know I have met __________ before!
Claudia: __________ too, but I can't remember where __________'ve seen __________.

☐ him – me – I – him ☐ them – they – I – them ☐ them – me – I – them

d Carine: Hi, Lola! How are __________? I heard __________ weren't at school yesterday.
Lola: But __________ was! The problem was that I left my essay at home and had to go back there to pick __________ up. When I got to school again, you weren't there anymore.

☐ you – you – I – it ☐ you – you – we – it ☐ you – I – I – them

7. The past two units made you reflect on the environment and on what we can do to protect it. You had the opportunity to talk and read about potential problems and also possible solutions to save our planet. What are they? Let's remember. Write P for Problems and S for Solutions.

a alternative sources of energy ☐
b chemical waste ☐
c deforestation ☐
d pollution ☐
e garbage separation ☐
f public transportation ☐

8. Now choose one of the problems or solutions from activity 7 and write what each photo represents.

a.

1

2

b.

3

d.

4

5

c.

e.

ART: SERGIO ONODERA/PHOTOS: PETER GINTER/THINKSTOCK (1); GEMENACOM/DREAMSTIME.COM (2); ISTOCKPHOTO/THINKSTOCK (3); DEHOOKS/DREAMSTIME.COM (4); COMSTOCK IMAGES/THINKSTOCK (5)

9. Match the columns appropriately to create meaningful statements.

a Don't text or read cell phone messages
b In classes, always ask questions
c "Listen carefully
d Please, speak slowly;
e Don't enter the fitting room now;

☐ there's a girl in there. She's trying on a nightgown.
☐ while you're on a date. It's impolite!
☐ to the story I have for you," said the little boy's grandma.
☐ when you have doubts.
☐ I don't understand what you're talking about.

✔ Check your answers on page 208.

JULIAN FINNEY/GETTY IMAGES

HOW INTELLIGENT ARE YOU?

NESTA UNIDADE VOCÊ IRÁ:

- **aprender sobre as múltiplas inteligências e as habilidades relacionadas a cada uma delas;**
- **estudar vocabulário relativo ao mercado de trabalho;**
- **identificar algumas das características de um diagrama;**
- **entender a composição de um questionário;**
- **estudar a ordem das palavras em uma frase;**
- **aprender a formar o plural das palavras.**

DAVID PAUL MORRIS/BLOOMBERG/GETTY IMAGES

unit 5

ROBSON FERNANDES/AGÊNCIA ESTADO

- **Você conhece essas pessoas? Quem são?**
- **Que habilidades elas possuem?**
- **Quais as diferenças e similaridades entre elas?**

Have Your Say

1 Look at the diagram below. What does it show?

[**diagram** /ˈdaɪəgræm/ noun [C] a drawing that explains something]

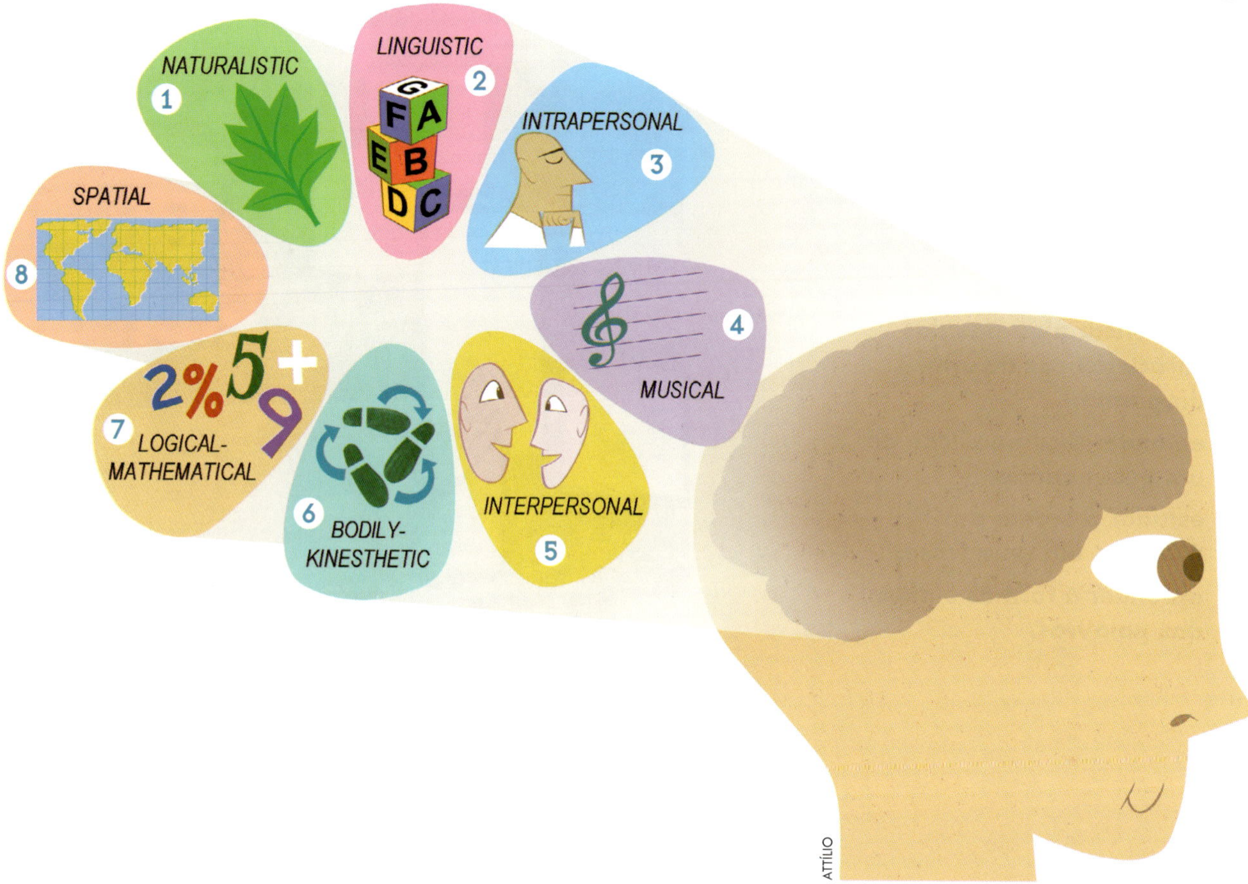

---

2 What activities are you really good at? Where do they fit in the diagram below?

---

3 Analyze the diagram in activity 1 and match each intelligence to its corresponding ability below. The first one is done for you.

- **a** ☐ to recognize and classify living things (flora and fauna)
- **b** [4] to recognize and produce sounds, rhythm, tone, and pitch
- **c** ☐ to recognize and deal with visual information
- **d** ☐ to understand and respond to other people's feelings
- **e** ☐ to understand one's own feelings and personality
- **f** ☐ to comprehend numbers, data, statistics, and logic
- **g** ☐ to understand words, sounds, and the use of language
- **h** ☐ to control body movements and to manipulate objects

TIP
Use your previous knowledge, the context, cognates, and textual clues to do the activity.

Reading Beyond the Words

1 Answer the questionnaire below to find out your strong intelligences.

Read the statements below. Write 1 next to the ones you agree with. Write 0 next to the ones you don't agree with.

Multiple Intelligences Questionnaire

- **A** ☐ I'm very sociable, and I like to be with my friends and family all the time.
- **B** ☐ Architecture, web design, desktop publishing are courses that interest me.
- **C** ☐ I prefer to read and / or to take notes to help me remember information.
- **D** ☐ I'm an independent thinker. I know my mind and my wishes.
- **E** ☐ I prefer to use rhymes and / or music to help me remember information.
- **F** ☐ I'm very concerned about endangered animals.
- **G** ☐ I'm interested in the areas of engineering and physics.
- **H** ☐ I definitely know myself well.
- **I** ☐ I can really understand other people's intentions and motivations.
- **J** ☐ I like to discover the connections between concepts.
- **K** ☐ I can remember new vocabulary easily.
- **L** ☐ I'm a member of green projects to help save our planet.
- **M** ☐ I'm a visually-oriented learner. Drawing tables and diagrams is a great learning strategy.
- **N** ☐ I'm very coordinated. Sports, dancing, or making things are some of my favorite hobbies.
- **O** ☐ I play different musical instruments. I like to compose and sing songs.
- **P** ☐ I like to think through problems while I walk or run.

RAFAEL GENTILE

Based on <www.bgfl.org>. Accessed on Oct 17, 2012.

2 In the chart below, add up the points you marked in the previous activity for each statement. The categories with 2 points express your strong intelligences.

Interpersonal	Intrapersonal	Linguistic	Bodily-kinesthetic
A. ______	D. ______	C. ______	N. ______
I. ______	H. ______	K. ______	P. ______
TOTAL: ______	TOTAL: ______	TOTAL: ______	TOTAL: ______

Naturalistic	Logical-mathematical	Musical	Spatial
F. ______	G. ______	E. ______	B. ______
L. ______	J. ______	O. ______	M. ______
TOTAL: ______	TOTAL: ______	TOTAL: ______	TOTAL: ______

RAFAEL GENTILE

3 Do you agree with the results? Discuss with a classmate.

4 Look at this chart with the results of someone's multiple intelligences test. Answer the questions below.

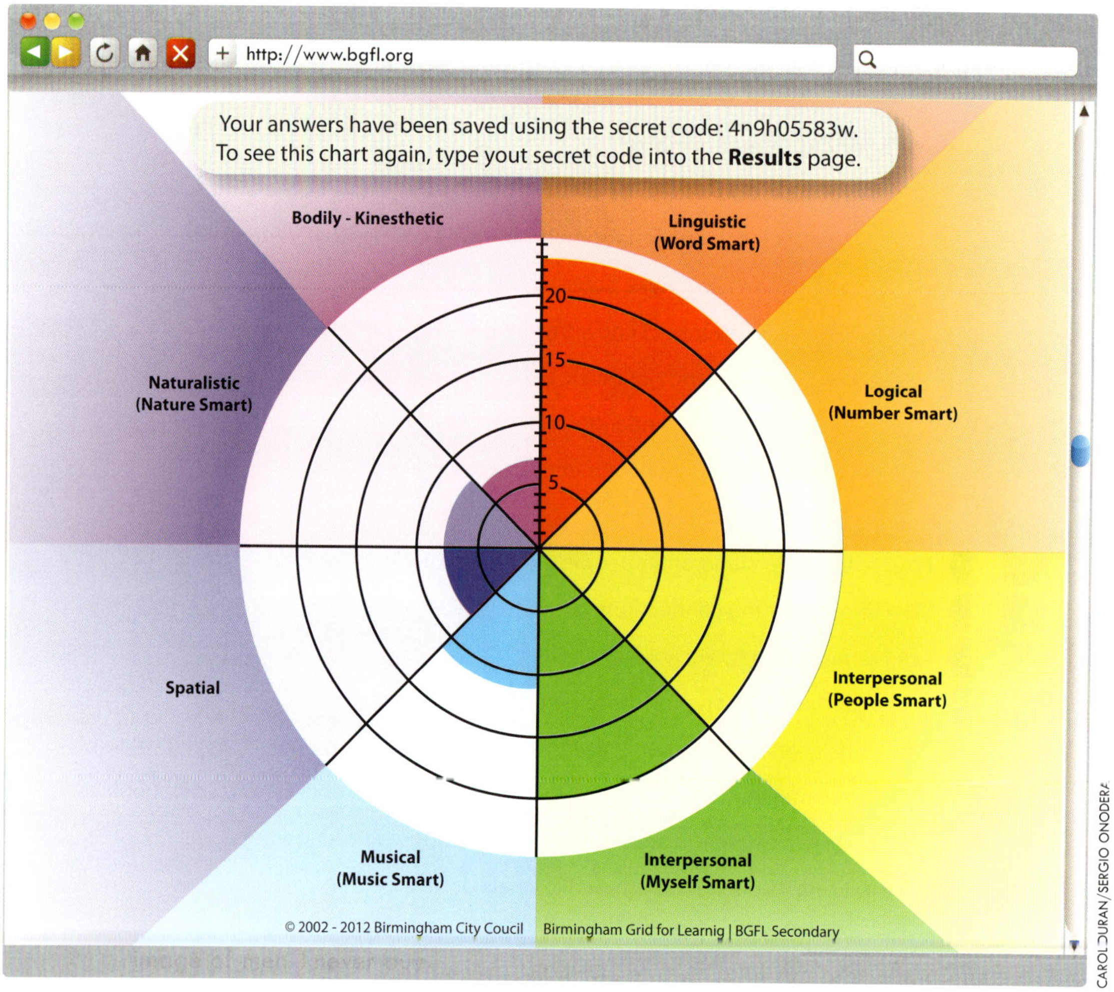

CAROL DURAN/SERGIO ONODERA

Extracted from <www.bgfl.org>. Accessed on Oct 17, 2012.

a What is the purpose of this chart?

b What do the colors and numbers indicate?

c Where was it taken from?

d Who produced it?

5 Study the results in the diagram. Which is the respondent's strongest intelligence? Which is the weakest?

6 Look at the different charts showing the results of some people's multiple intelligences tests. Match each of them to their identification: (1) a column bar chart, (2) a line chart, (3) a pie chart.

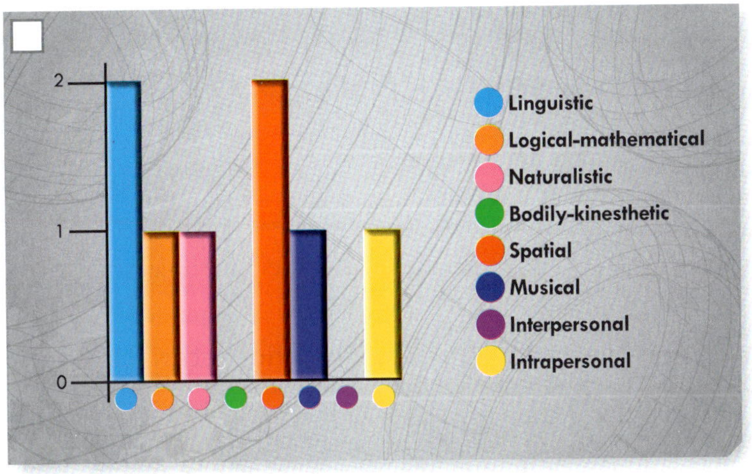

Natural Sciences & Math

TIP

Charts are a specific type of diagram. They represent numerical or qualitative information in a visual way.

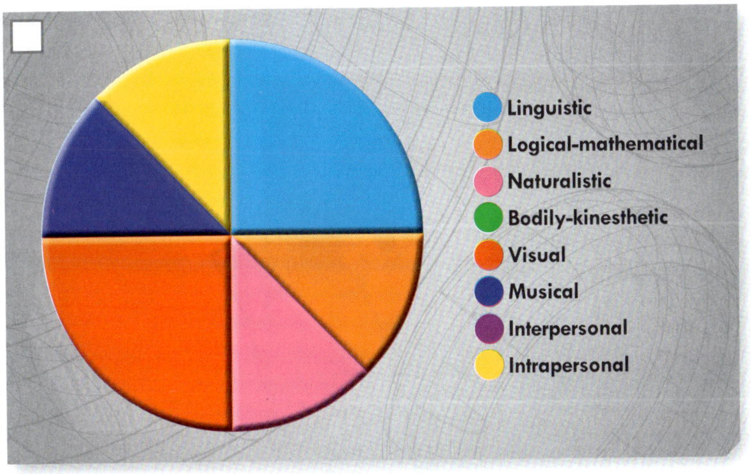

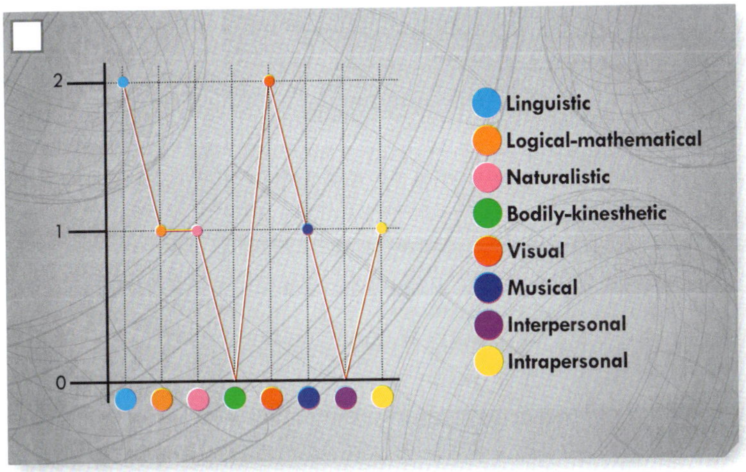

ARTS: ROBERTA BENITES

7 Based on the questionnaire you answered on page 89, create a chart of your results. Share it with the rest of the class.

Genre Analysis

1 Check the characteristics that define a questionnaire.

A questionnaire:

a ☐ can be a group of questions to collect information about a specific subject.

b ☐ is written in a fixed sequence: introduction, body, and conclusion.

c ☐ is about a specific subject.

d ☐ is a list of reminders of things to do.

e ☐ can be a group of statements to collect information about a specific subject.

2 Read the questionnaire on page 89 again. Which of the characteristics marked above can you find there?

____

3 Check the correct statements about diagrams.

A diagram:

a ☐ usually explores space in order to express information in a visual way.

b ☐ is an ironic text about politicians, political parties, etc.

c ☐ makes use of verbal and non-verbal information to express meaning.

d ☐ displays information in a compact way to facilitate comprehension.

e ☐ is organized in questions with multiple-choice answers or in incomplete statements.

4 Go back to the diagram on page 90. Which characteristics of diagrams listed in activity 3 can you find?

____

Vocabulary

1 Look at the multiple intelligences questionnaire on page 89. Find cognates and write them in the table according to their corresponding word classes.

Verb	Noun	Adjective	Adverb

2 Read the statements from the questionnaire on page 89. Match the words / expressions in blue to their corresponding definitions.

a Architecture, web design, and **desktop publishing** are courses that interest me.

b I'm an independent thinker. I know my mind and my **wishes**.

c I'm very concerned about **endangered** animals.

d **Drawing** tables and diagrams is a great learning strategy.

e I like to **think through** problems while I walk or run.

☐ desires, things you want for yourself

☐ to consider the facts about something in an organized way

☐ a type of animal that may soon become extinct

☐ the activity or ability of making pictures with a pen or pencil

☐ the production of printed material with the use of a computer word editor, for example

TIP

Be careful with *false* cognates. They are English words that look similar to Portuguese words, but have different meanings.
actually – na verdade
library – biblioteca
lunch – almoço
push – empurrar

3 Look at the professions below and match them to each type of intelligence. Some of them can be used more than once.

accountant | actor | administrator | architect | biologist | computer programmer | counselor | dancer | designer | DJ | English teacher | geologist | journalist | mathematician | mechanic | musician | nurse | personal trainer | philosopher | pilot | politician | salesperson | secretary | singer | veterinarian | writer

Intelligence	Careers
Linguistic	
Spatial	
Interpersonal	
Bodily-kinesthetic	
Logical-mathematical	
Intrapersonal	
Naturalistic	
Musical	

Grammar

1 Complete the information in the diagram below.

TIP
A modifier describes and / or adds information to a word.

Modifiers

Word Order in English

different musical instruments

Modifiers → Head of the group

Word Order in Portuguese

instrumentos **musicais variados**

Head of the group ← Modifiers

In English, modifiers come ________________ the head of a group of words.

In Portuguese, modifiers usually come ________________ the head of a group of words.

RAFAEL GENTILE

2 In the examples below, the heads of the groups of words are highlighted. Underline their modifier(s).

a I'm aware of my personal and learning **weaknesses**, so I always try to have more control over them.

b I'm a visually-oriented **learner**. Drawing tables and diagrams is my favorite learning **strategy**.

c I don't like to deal with mathematical **figures** and statistical **data**.

3 Read these sentences from the questionnaire and circle the words in the plural.

"I'm very sociable, and I like to be with my friends and family all the time."

"I'm an independent thinker. I know my mind and my wishes."

"[…] Drawing tables and diagrams is a great learning strategy."

RAFAEL GENTILE

4 Now answer the questions.

a Are the words with plural endings nouns or verbs? ________________

b Which letters are used to form plurals in the examples above? ________________

c Do adjectives have a plural form in English? ________________

In Other Words

Ordem das palavras

A ordem das palavras em inglês (substantivo e seus modificadores) é diferente da sequência em português. Por exemplo, na frase "I play different musical instruments", a ordem das palavras correspondentes a *different musical instruments* será bem diferente em português (instrumentos musicais variados).

Procure sempre identificar o substantivo para associá-lo a seus modificadores (adjetivos, verbos, artigos, etc.) quando fizer uso do inglês em suas interações, tanto na modalidade oral quanto na escrita.

A estratégia de identificar as classes de palavras pode se configurar em uma ajuda importante.

- Adjetivos (*adjectives*) descrevem ideias, pessoas e objetos.

  big; difficult; independent

- Advérbios (*adverbs*) modificam verbos, adjetivos e outros advérbios.

  always; normally; quickly

- Conjunções (*conjunctions*) / palavras de ligação (*linking words*) estabelecem as relações entre as ideias de um texto.

  and; because; but

- Interjeições (*interjections*) expressam emoção e o sentimento de quem fala ou escreve.

  Dear me!; Poor him!

- Substantivos (*nouns*) nomeiam ideias, pessoas, países, objetos.

  equality; Peter; England; book

- Preposições (*prepositions*) estabelecem relações entre as palavras em uma frase.

  at; from; on

- Pronomes (*pronouns*) referem-se a substantivos ou os substituem para evitar repetição.

  she; that; who

- Verbos (*verbs*) expressam ação (*action verbs*); estado (*state verbs*) ou ligam o sujeito à sua qualidade (*linking verbs*).

  walk (*action verb*); love (*state verb*); sound (*linking verbs*)

O plural dos substantivos

O plural de palavras em inglês é formado da seguinte maneira:

- Na maior parte dos casos, acrescenta-se ***-s*** aos substantivos:

  diagram – diagrams; lesson – lessons; piano – pianos; nurse – nurses

- Substantivos terminados em ***-s***; ***-ss***; ***-sh***; ***-ch***; ***-x*** recebem ***-es***:

  box – boxes; bus – buses; dish – dishes; watch – watches; weakness – weaknesses

- Substantivos terminados em consoante seguida de ***-y*** trocam o ***-y*** por ***-i*** e recebem a terminação ***-es***:

  activity – activities; family – families; strategy – strategies

- Substantivos terminados em vogal seguida de ***-y*** apenas recebem o ***-s***:

  day – days; way – ways

- Acrescenta-se ***-es*** a alguns substantivos terminados em ***-o***:

  hero – heroes; potato – potatoes

  - Palavras que admitem ambas as formas:

    mosquito – mosquitos / mosquitoes; volcano – volcanos / volcanoes

- Muitos substantivos terminados em ***-f*** ou ***-fe*** recebem a terminação ***-ves***:

  knife – knives; scarf – scarves; wife – wives

- Alguns substantivos possuem forma de plural irregular:

  child – **children**
  man – **men**
  mouse – **mice**
  person – **people**
  tooth – **teeth**
  woman – **women**

Lembre-se de que em inglês os adjetivos não têm plural.

Practice Makes Perfect

1 For each profession below, circle the head and underline the modifier.

- airplane pilot
- ballet dancer
- career counselor
- electrical engineer
- English teacher
- web designer

2 Study the underlined groups of words in the excerpt below. In your notebook, draw diagrams to show their word order (use the example on page 95).

<u>The logical-mathematical intelligence</u> involves the capacity to think conceptually in <u>logical and numerical patterns</u> making connections between pieces of information. Learners who are good at it are always curious about the world around them, ask lots of questions and like to investigate problems scientifically. [...] they like to work with <u>abstract concepts</u> to discover the relationship of each to the other and to perform <u>complex mathematical calculations</u>.

RAFAEL GENTILE

Adapted from GARDNER, Howard. *Frames of Mind: The Theory of Multiple Intelligences*. New York: Basic Books, 1983.

3 Read another excerpt about multiple intelligences. Write the plural form of the nouns in parentheses.

www.tecweb.org

[...] **Linguistic** – using ________ (word) effectively. These ________ (learner) like reading, taking notes in their ________ (class), making up poetry or ________ (story).

Interpersonal – understanding, interacting with others. These ________ (student) learn through interaction. They like group ________ (activity), ________ (seminar), ________ (debate), ________ (interview).

Logical-Mathematical – reasoning, calculating. ________ (Person) who excel in this intelligence like to experiment, solve ________ (puzzle), play with logic ________ (game), read about ________ (investigation), and solve ________ (mystery).

RAFAEL GENTILE

Adapted from <www.tecweb.org>. Accessed on Oct 18, 2012.

4 Write the words from the previous activity in the correct column according to the plural endings.

-s	-ies	-es	Irregular

The Way It Sounds

game show /geɪm ʃoʊ/ noun [C] a television show in which people play games or answer questions in order to win prizes

1 Listen to the introduction of a game show. What is the focus of today's program? Check the correct option.

10

- **a** ☐ An academic report about multiple intelligences.
- **b** ☐ A quiz on multiple intelligences.
- **c** ☐ A brief report about multiple intelligences.

2 Read the questions from the game show and check the correct answers.

Question 1

This great Brazilian racing driver was intelligent in so many ways, especially visual intelligence. He is still recognized for his exceptional talent and determination. Who is he?

- ○ César Cielo.
- ○ Gustavo Kuerten, or "Guga".
- ○ Ayrton Senna.

Question 2

People who have this type of intelligence are able to control their body and handle objects skillfully. Which intelligence is it?

- ○ Body smart.
- ○ Picture smart.
- ○ Word smart.

Question 3

This brilliant Brazilian athlete is the winner of two Olympic medals for sailing. Unfortunately, because of a serious accident he had one of his legs amputated. Who is he?

- ○ Lars Grael.
- ○ Bruno Fontes.
- ○ Amyr Klink.

RAFAEL GENTILE

3 Now listen to the complete game show and check your answers.

11

4 Listen to the game show once more and answer the questions below.

12

a What is the name of the game show host?

☐ Alan Price. ☐ Jayden Price. ☐ Jordan Price.

b Who answered the second question?

☐ Emily. ☐ Leah. ☐ Nobody.

c Who is the winner of the game?

☐ Emily. ☐ Jayden. ☐ Leah.

TalkActive

Play the game *Find someone who.*

Preparation

- Check the results of the questionnaire you answered on page 89.
- Complete the information below about yourself.

- My strongest intelligences: ______________________________
- Things I'm good at: ______________________________
- My favorite subjects: ______________________________
- My hobbies: ______________________________

ROBERTA BENITES

The game

- Go around your classroom and find someone who has strong intelligences similar to yours.
- When you find three people who have the same intelligence(s) as you, sit together as a group.
- Talk to your group about your hobbies and your favorite subjects. What do you have in common? Take notes.

ROBERTA BENITES

Sharing

- Share your findings with your class. List the things your group has in common. Then list the things that are different or unique to just one or two members of the group.

Self-assessment

MAURO SOUZA

AO FINAL DESTA UNIDADE, JÁ SOU CAPAZ DE	
reconhecer os diferentes tipos de inteligência.	
identificar as características de questionários.	
identificar as características de diagramas.	
reconhecer e usar vocabulário relacionado a profissões.	
reconhecer e usar a ordem das palavras na oração (substantivos e modificadores) de maneira correta.	
reconhecer e usar o plural dos substantivos.	

Se você deixou de marcar algum dos itens na tabela de autoavaliação, procure no *site* deste livro atividades extras que o ajudem a praticar e consolidar os tópicos desta unidade.

Going Beyond

Movie

- *Senna*. 2010. Documentary. About the life and work of the triple world champion, his achievements on the track, and his quest for perfection.

Website

- Go to the following site to take a test on multiple intelligences: <www.bgfl.org/custom/resources_ftp/client_ftp/ks3/ict/multiple_int/questions/questions.cfm>. Copy down the code that identifies your diagram results. Print them out. Share them with your classmates. Accessed on Nov 14, 2012.

5

Objeto educacional digital

BANANASTOCK/MARS

STUDY SKILLS AND STRATEGIES

NESTA UNIDADE VOCÊ IRÁ:

- utilizar diferentes estratégias de aprendizagem;
- usar vocabulário relacionado a hábitos de estudo;
- identificar as características de um guia didático;
- entender a formação e as funções de advérbios;
- estudar formação de palavras por sufixação;
- ouvir e corrigir informações sobre uma palestra;
- conduzir uma entrevista informal.

CORBIS/MARS

unit 6

ROB LEWINE/GETTY IMAGES

- Que hábitos de estudo as fotos estão mostrando?
- Você acha que as pessoas das fotos aprendem da mesma maneira?
- De que maneira você estuda?

Have Your Say

1 Look at the following rooms. Check the one that is appropriate for studying at home.

MAURO SOUZA

2 Discuss and justify your choice in activity 1. What are the characteristics of an appropriate place for studying?

3 Check the advantages of a well-organized study room.

- **a** ☐ The student is free from distraction.
- **b** ☐ The student is less productive.
- **c** ☐ It helps the student not to waste time.
- **d** ☐ It helps the student focus on priorities.
- **e** ☐ It helps the student concentrate.

4 Look at the photos below. Then answer the questions and discuss your answers with a classmate.

RYAN MCVAY/THINKSTOCK

PURESTOCK/THINKSTOCK

- **a** In your opinion, are these places appropriate for studying? Why?
- **b** What learning strategies are the people in the photos using?
- **c** Do you use these strategies to learn English? Why?

Reading Beyond the Words

1 Do you have any study strategies for learning English? What are they? Discuss.

2 Read the text below and check if your strategies are mentioned.

http://www.nclrc.org

NCLRC THE ESSENTIAL OF LANGUAGE TEACHING

Home

PRINCIPLES

- What language teaching is
- Teaching goals and methods
- Planning a lesson
- Motivating learners
  - Understanding Language Acquisition
  - Promoting Engagement in Learning
  - Using Learning Strategies
  - Resources
- Assessing learning

PRACTICE

- Teaching grammar
- Teaching listening
- Teaching speaking
- Teaching reading
- Teaching writing
- Teaching culture

Achieving Success with Learning Strategies

Students who are learning a language have two kinds of knowledge working for them:

- their knowledge of their first language;
- their awareness of learning strategies.

Differences in ability, motivation, or effort explain partially why students are not similar. A major difference is how they use learning strategies. Classroom research demonstrates how learning strategies can help language learning:

- good learners can identify the best strategy for a specific task; inefficient learners have difficulty deciding on one;
- good learners are flexible and adopt a different strategy if the first one doesn't work; inefficient learners have a limited variety of strategies and stay with the first one even when it doesn't work;
- good learners have confidence in their learning ability; inefficient learners don't;
- good learners expect success, achieve success, and become more motivated; inefficient learners expect to do badly, are unsuccessful, and lose motivation.

Teaching learning strategies shows students that their success is the result of the way they manage learning. Most students can learn how to use strategies more effectively. When it happens, they become more independent, they take more responsibility for their own learning, and their motivation increases. [...]

Adapted from <www.nclrc.org>. Accessed on Oct 19, 2012.

3 "Achieving Success with Learning Strategies" is:

a ☐ a home page about learning strategies.

b ☐ a blog post about learning strategies.

c ☐ an educational guide on learning strategies.

d ☐ an encyclopedia entry on learning strategies.

4 The guide is composed of three paragraphs. Match each paragraph to its main topic.

☐ distinctions between good and inefficient learners

☐ advantages all language learners have in common

☐ advantages of teaching learning strategies

5 Classify the sentences into the two categories below.

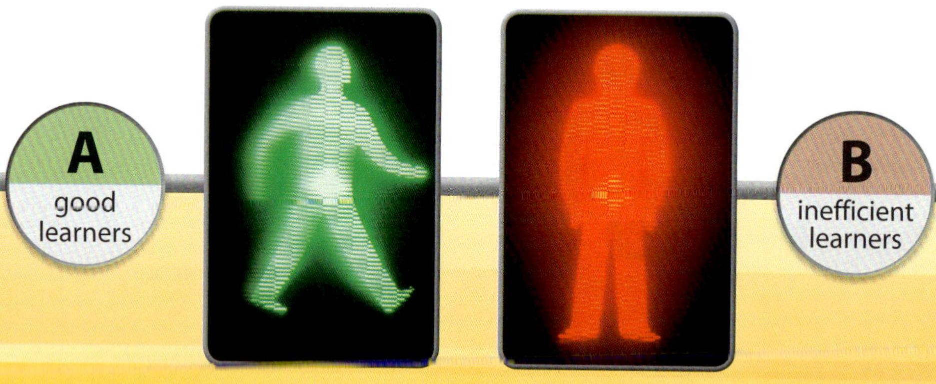

a ☐ They believe in their ability to learn a language.

b ☐ They persist with a strategy independently of their result.

c ☐ They are conscious of the strategies they use for learning.

d ☐ They perform badly and feel discouraged because of it.

e ☐ They don't take responsibility for their learning.

ART: RAFAEL GENTILE; PHOTOS: FUSE/THINKSTOCK

6 What are your strengths as an English learner? What can you improve? How?

____

____

____

7 Can you manage your learning process well? Check the options that are true for you.

a ☐ I always use different strategies for different tasks.

b ☐ I organize my time.

c ☐ I sometimes ask friends to study with me.

d ☐ I always use the suggestions in the Going Beyond section in this book.

e ☐ I test myself to help me decide what I need to study more.

f ☐ I learn a lot from the Engage activities in this book.

8 Discuss your study habits with a partner.

Genre Analysis

1 Complete the sentences below about the educational guide on page 105. Use the features below.

authorship   intended audience   purpose   theme

a "English teachers" is the ____________________

b "The NCLRC (a Language Resource Center)" is the ____________________

c "Learning strategies" is the ____________________

d "To teach about learning strategies" is the ____________________

2 Check the basic characteristics of an educational guide.

a ☐ Its main purpose is clearly indicated in the title.

b ☐ It sometimes contains sequences of examples indicated by bullets.

c ☐ Words are usually repeated to clarify meaning.

d ☐ It is often written in informal language and expresses an opinion.

e ☐ It uses online resources like sections organized in different webpages.

f ☐ It's always written by a teacher.

3 Circle the correct option to complete the sentence below.

The verbs in an educational guide are usually in the **past** / **present** tense.

Vocabulary

1 Match each reading strategy to what the following people say about them. The first one is done for you.

a making inferences
b scanning
c using cognates
d using context
e using previous knowledge
f using textual clues
g using verbal and non-verbal clues

ART: ERIKA ONODERA; PHOTOS: DARRINHENRY/DREAMSTIME.COM / CHRISTIAN NASCA/ISTOCKPHOTO/THINKSTOCK (1); SAM ROYDS/THINKSTOCK (2); UPTALL/DREAMSTIME.COM (3); JUPITERIMAGES/POLKA DOT RF/THINKSTOCK (4); HUNTSTOCK/THINKSTOCK (5); WAVEBREAK MEDIA/THINKSTOCK (6); AVAVA/DREAMSTIME.COM (7)

2 In the lists below, underline the strategies you use. Then circle the ones you intend to incorporate into your study habits.

Vocabulary development strategies	Reading comprehension strategies
associating words to images	skimming – scanning
identifying prefixes and suffixes in words	making inferences
keeping a glossary	using cognates
learning definitions of words	using previous knowledge
learning words and their synonyms	using textual clues
using a dictionary	using verbal and non-verbal information

RAFAEL GENTILE

3 Look at the French text below. Use the strategies from activity 2 to answer the questions.

Languages

a What kind of text is it?

b What's the name of the company that produces the jam?

c How do you say "strawberries" in French?

d What cognates are there in the text?

e What's the general message of the text?

f What does "rabais" mean?

ART: RAFAEL GENTILE/ROBERTA BENITES; PHOTOS: ANDY CRAWFORD/DORLING KINDERSLEY RF/THINKSTOCK/VASILY PINDYURIN/HEMERA/THINKSTOCK

4 What strategies did you use to answer questions **a** to **f**?

Grammar

1 Study the statements and dictionary entries below. Then circle the correct options to complete them.

Good learners study independently and autonomously.

They are independent and autonomous learners.

Most students can successfully learn how to use different learning strategies.

Successful students use different learning strategies for different purposes.

adjective /ˈædʒəktɪv/ noun [C] a word used for describing a noun or pronoun

adverb /ˈædˌvɜrb/ noun [C] a word used for describing a verb, an adjective, another adverb, or a whole sentence

a The words highlighted in blue are **adjectives / adverbs**.

b The words highlighted in green are **adjectives / adverbs**.

2 Study the highlighted words in activity 1 again to complete the sentence below.

You can form adverbs from ______________ by adding ______________ at the end of the word.

3 Change adjectives into adverbs by adding *-ly*.

a active ______________

b certain ______________

c partial ______________

d quick ______________

e careful ______________

f poor ______________

4 Choose three adverbs from the previous activity and write three true sentences about you or a classmate.

____

____

____

5 Discuss these questions about study habits.

a Do you participate actively in class discussions?

b Do you revise your texts carefully after you finish writing?

c If you perform poorly in an activity, do you study the topic again?

d Can you use different learning strategies effectively?

e Do you quickly review the lessons of the day before you do your homework?

f Are you a good learner? Why?

In Other Words

Advérbios

Os advérbios têm a mesma função em inglês e em português. Modificam um verbo, um adjetivo, outro advérbio ou uma frase completa.

Forma:

- Acrescenta-se *-ly* ao final do adjetivo.

  beautiful – beautiful**ly**; perfect – perfect**ly**

- Nos adjetivos terminados em *-y*, troque o *-y* por *-i* antes de acrescentar *-ly*.

  easy – eas**ily**; happy – happ**ily**

- Nos adjetivos terminados em *-le*, retire o *-e* antes de acrescentar o *-y*.

  comfortable – comfortab**ly**; possible – possib**ly**

- Nos adjetivos terminados em *-ic*, acrescente *-ally*.

  basic – basic**ally**; fantastic – fantastic**ally**

Tipos:

- Adverbs of manner

  actively, quickly, easily, independently, carefully, poorly

- Adverbs of place

  above, below, here, there, near, far (from)

- Adverbs of time

  today, yesterday, now, early, late, last, next, soon, ago

- Adverbs of duration

  temporarily, shortly, indefinitely, permanently, forever

- Adverbs of degree

  very, almost, extremely, greatly, partially, strongly, totally

- Adverbs of probability

  possibly, perhaps, maybe, almost, certainly, definitely

Formação de palavras por sufixação

Além da terminação *-ly*, que forma advérbios a partir de adjetivos, há vários outros sufixos formadores de novas palavras. Veja os exemplos do quadro abaixo.

O(s) sufixo(s)	a partir de	forma(m)	que indicam
-er -or	**verbos** learn teach act revise	**substantivos** learner teacher actor revisor	**aquele que faz**
-ment	**verbos** announce develop entertain involve	**substantivos** announcement development entertainment involvement	**um conceito**
-ness	**adjetivos** cute dark happy aware	**substantivos abstratos** cuteness darkness happiness awareness	**um estado ou sentimento**
-less	**substantivos** clue hope home care	**adjetivos** clueless hopeless homeless careless	**ausência de**
-ful	**substantivos** success care delight help	**adjetivos** successful careful delightful helpful	**abundância de**
-ish -an -ian -ese	**substantivos** England Mexico Brazil Portugal	**adjetivos** English Mexican Brazilian Portuguese	**nacionalidade**

Practice Makes Perfect

1 Read the statements below and do the activities that follow.

- Always create meaningful examples of grammar structures.
- Students can achieve learning engagement by assessing their own progress.
- Keeping good study habits help you learn more efficiently.
- It's useless to study one hour before a test.
- Don't let shyness stop you from speaking in front of your class.
- My cousin wants to be a math teacher, but I want to be an engineer.
- Jack wants to be a professional tennis player.

TIP

Suffixes are important textual clues to discover word classes. Knowing the class of a word can help you read, write, speak, and listen.

a Underline the words with suffixes in the sentences above.

b Write the underlined words according to their word classes.

Adjective(s): ____________________

Adverb(s): ____________________

Noun(s): ____________________

2 Turn the adjectives below into adverbs. The first one is done for you.

a certain: certainly

b easy: ____________________

c frequent: ____________________

d immediate: ____________________

e ironic: ____________________

f probable: ____________________

3 Give some studying suggestions to your classmates. Use the adverbs you formed in the previous activity and a dictionary if necessary.

a Develop study habits to learn English more easily.

b ____________________

c ____________________

d ____________________

e ____________________

f ____________________

The Way It Sounds

1 Check the pieces of advice you expect to hear in a lecture about study skills.

- [ ] analyze how you learn
- [ ] do your homework
- [ ] go to your classes
- [ ] organize to-do lists
- [ ] pay attention in your classes
- [ ] read visual aids carefully
- [ ] study regularly
- [ ] test yourself regularly

2 Listen to the study skills lecture carefully. Check your answers in activity 1.

13

3 Listen to the lecture once more and correct the sentences below.

14

[**skip** /skɪp/ verb to avoid doing something]

a The number two reason students do inefficiently is because they skip classes.

____

b Test yourself regularly and, based on the results, organize to-do lists.

____

c Study on the night before a test.

____

d Reading visual aids carefully can help you memorize subjects more easily.

____

4 Analyze the corrected sentences in the previous activity and answer the questions.

a Do you agree with statement **a**? Why?

____

b Are these strategies effective for you? Which ones? Justify your answer.

____

5 Think about the last category in the lecture: using web resources. Write some study strategies you can use to learn English to include in this category.

____

____

____

____

Put It in Writing

Plan your writing.

What to write: Tips for successful learning.

Purpose: To come up with strategies that can help you learn English.

Audience: Your classmates.

Complete the titles of the tips with the expressions below.

great photography | saving money | speaking in public

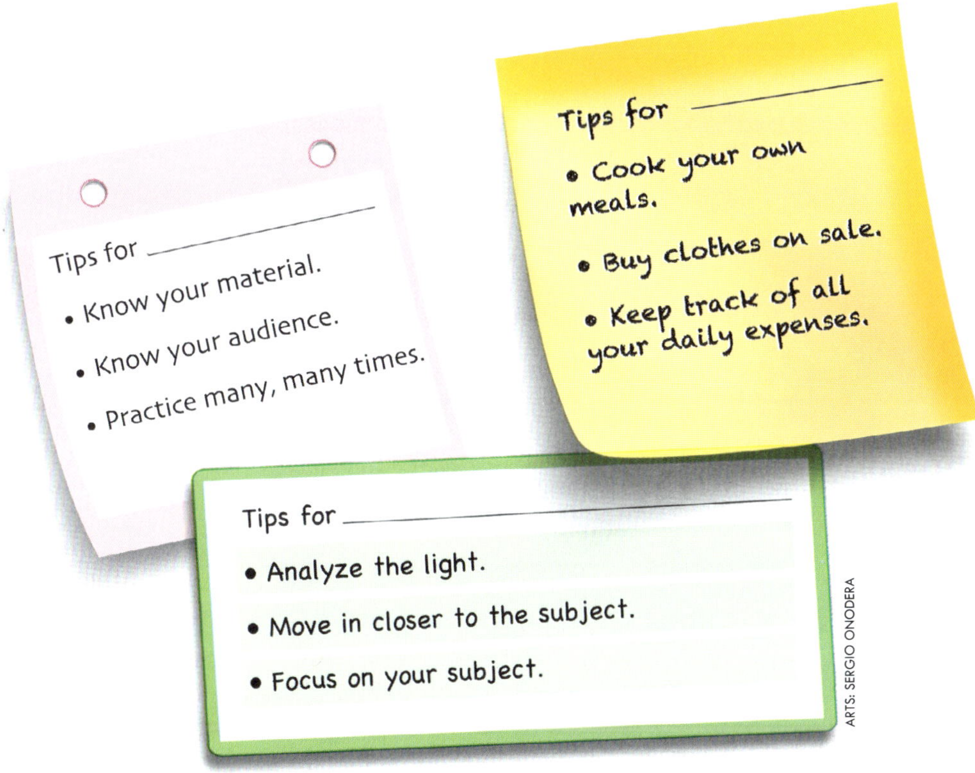

ARTS: SERGIO ONODERA

Brainstorm some ideas and make a list with the title "Tips for effective English learning."

Use the checklist below to revise your list.

		Yes	No
1	It respects the characteristics of the genre.		
2	It meets my writing objectives.		
3	The language is appropriate to my audience.		
4	The text uses good grammar and punctuation.		

- If you checked *no* in any topic above, rewrite your email.

Publish your tips.

- Post your tips on the class bulletin board.

TalkActive

Interview a classmate about his / her study strategies.

Preparation

- Use the tips you created on the previous page. Change them into questions. Study the examples below.

Tips	Questions
Always use reading strategies.	Do you always use reading strategies?
Actively participate in teamwork.	Do you actively participate in teamwork?

- Create other questions for the interview.

The interview

- Interview your classmate. Use the options to check your classmate's answers.

Questions	Always	Sometimes	Never
1			
2			
3			
4			
5			
6			
7			

Sharing

- Share what you found out in your interview with another classmate. Were you surprised? Why (not)?

TIP

How to conduct the interview:
- **prepare your questions carefully.**
- **don't interrupt your classmate.**
- **be nice and understanding.**
- **always give your classmate time to answer.**
- **at the end, thank your classmate for his / her time.**

Self-assessment

MAURO SOUZA

AO FINAL DESTA UNIDADE, JÁ SOU CAPAZ DE	
reconhecer e utilizar diferentes estratégias de aprendizagem.	
reconhecer e usar vocabulário relacionado a hábitos de estudo.	
identificar as características de um *educational guide*.	
reconhecer e utilizar vários tipos de advérbios.	
reconhecer e usar a formação de palavras por sufixação.	
ouvir e compreender uma palestra sobre hábitos de estudo.	
conduzir uma entrevista informal.	

Se você deixou de marcar algum dos itens na tabela de autoavaliação, procure no *site* deste livro atividades extras que o ajudem a praticar e consolidar os tópicos desta unidade.

Going Beyond

Movie

- *Capitães da areia*. 2011. Drama. Based on the book by Jorge Amado. The movie is about a gang of street kids in Salvador, Bahia. Their adventures show how the kids develop strategies to deal with their adversities. Read more at: <www.imdb.com>.

Website

- Take a study skills survey at <www.angelo.edu/services/first_year_experience/study_skills> (accessed on Oct 30, 2012) and learn more about managing your own learning.

6

Objeto educacional digital

Tour Guide

What is it like to be a tour guide? Read the fact file below.

ART: RAFAEL GENTILE; PHOTO: PAUL SPRINGETT 05/ALAMY/GLOW IMAGES

TOUR GUIDE FACT FILE	
Job description	• Show popular attractions to tourists; • Organize and lead tours or cruises with groups of tourists; • Share historical facts, dates, and anecdotes with visitors in a fun way; • Translate or interpret.
Tour guides work for	• Tour and travel guide companies, cruise lines, visitors' bureaus, and hotels as seasonal workers, independent contractors, or full-time employees.
Advantages	• Can work as freelancers or full-time employees; • Can visit all the best locations around the world; • Have accommodation, meals, and transport paid for by the company; • Are constantly learning about all different destinations.
Disadvantages	• Have lots of responsibility looking after a large group of people; • Need to do a lot of research and to memorize all the information about the places; • Spend a lot of time away from home; • Have long working hours.
Professional options	• Tour guides can choose different types of tourism: adventure, archeological, ecotourism, historical, recreational, artistic, architectural, culinary, religious, etc.

Based on <www.allaboutcareers.com>, <http://education-portal.com>, and <www.jobmonkey.com>. Accessed on Nov 9, 2012.

Do you have the key skills to become a tour guide? Check YES or NO in the table below.

Are you:	Yes	No
a friendly, social person?		
happy being away from home for long periods of time?		
a leader?		
able to do lots of reading and research to plan your tours?		
organized and patient?		
a good storyteller and public speaker?		
calm in an emergency situation?		

Would you like to become a tour guide? Why?

FACT FILES (part III)

Writing a fact file

What to write: A cool job fact file.

Purpose: To share information about some jobs students might be interested in.

Audience: Your group or your school community.

Brainstorming and planning

Think of cool jobs and find out more about them. Write them down in the space below.

✔ For some tips, check: <www.cooljobs.com/>.

ROBERTA BENITES

TIP

Use different online search engines to find more results.
Think of keywords or phrases to use in your search:
"Biker photographer job description"
"Scuba diving instructor profile"
"What does an assistant director do?"

Researching

Choose one job for your fact file.

In your notebook, write what you know about the job you chose.

Research to find out more about the job. Take notes of key facts.

Remember!

Fact files...
- bring key facts about a specific event, person, or place;
- inform people about a specific subject;
- are organized in topics.

RAFAEL GENTILE

Writing a draft

Write a draft of your fact file.

SELF-STUDY units 5-6

1. In Unit 6, you read an educational guide on learning strategies. Keep on reflecting on ways to improve your learning by reading the article below. Then complete it with the words from the boxes.

doing | groups | hearing | language | see | self-study | work

Education & The Brain

What Are Learning Styles?

Learning styles refer to the different ways that different people are best able to learn new information. While traditional forms of education have only focused on one or two different learning styles, newer approaches to education have introduced a greater focus on utilizing multiple learning styles to ensure that different students can learn as effectively as possible.

Visual (or spatial) learning refers to people who learn most effectively through what they can ________________. Visual learners also typically benefit a great deal from visual aids such as graphs, charts, pictures, and diagrams.

Aural (or auditory-musical) learners are best able to learn through ________________ material. These types of learners benefit from oral lectures and often read aloud to themselves when covering material in a textbook.

Verbal (or linguistic) learners typically learn best through ________________, both through listening and reading. These types of learners benefit a great deal from language and often excel in classes where language is stressed, such as English and reading.

Physical (or kinesthetic) learners often learn best through ________________ things physically. These types of learners may do well in science classes with a great deal of lab work, or in sports and other physical activities.

Logical (or mathematical) learners tend to learn through logical understanding of how things ________________ and relate. These types of learners often make lists and tend to excel at math and science.

Social learners learn well in ________________, either in full class or small group discussions, while solitary learners tend to learn best through ________________ or by working alone.

38 | Brain Magazine

SERGIO ONODERA

Adapted from <www.wisegeek.com>. Accessed on Nov 4, 2012.

2. Words are very important for effective communication. Learning new vocabulary is one of the biggest challenges in learning English.
Underline the heads of the groups of words and rewrite the statements to insert the modifiers in parentheses. Go back to pages 95, 96 and 98 to review word order in English.

a The microwave is a kitchen appliance. (very useful)

The microwave is a very useful kitchen appliance.

b My gardener uses special tools to take care of these flowers. (garden)

______

c I left my shoes back home. (golf)

______

d Why did the Sanders bring their sweet baby to the party? (7-month-old)

______

e Andrea was wearing an amazing dress! (evening)

______

f He dreamed of becoming a world champion. (boxing)

______

3. Go back to pages 95, 97 and 98 to revise what you've already studied on the topic. What words from the lists below do you already know? Use a dictionary to look up the unfamiliar ones.
Cross the odd word out of each group of nouns and provide their plural. Take a look at item **a** as a reference.

a box | watch | glass | ~~scarf~~

two boxes
three watches
ten glasses
two scarves

b bus | article | wardrobe | drugstore

three ______
two ______
two ______
three ______

c child | city | tooth | mouse

three ______
two ______
five ______
four ______

d radio | hero | potato | tomato

two ______
four ______
three ______
five ______

4. As you learned in Unit 6, adverbs are used to add information about time, place, manner, frequency, or cause. In our everyday lives we use adverbs to describe when, where, how, or how often something happens.
Read the statements below related to typical social interactions. Then underline the adverbs in the sentences and write what they express: degree, duration, frequency, manner, or time. If you need to review the adverbs, refer back to pages 110, 111 and 113.

a I have to do something about this quickly. ____________________

b The children are playing outside. ____________________

c She went out briefly. ____________________

d I totally agree with you. ____________________

e We need to edit these files immediately. ____________________

f I frequently do something to help him. ____________________

5. When we add a suffix to a word, we form a new word. By doing that, we usually learn new words from words we already know.
Improve your vocabulary and learn more about word formation by doing the activity that follows. Match the suffixes to complete the nouns and adjectives in the statements. If you need extra help, go back to unit 6 to get more information on this topic.

a *-ful*	☐ Some learners can be more practical and care__________ than others.
b *-ment*	☐ If you overemphasize intuition, you may make care__________ mistakes in calculations or hands-on work.
c *-less*	☐ People tend to be involved with others to avoid loneli__________.
d *-ese*	☐ The develop__________ of all your mental capacities can help you become a better professional.
e *-ness*	☐ The Chin__________ are one of the biggest producers of robots in the world.

6. Differently from adverbs, adjectives are used to describe the quality of people, animals and things. Refer back to the Grammar Sections in units 5 and 6 to learn more about the use of adjectives and adverbs. Now, do the activity that follows. Write "ADJ" for adjectives and "ADV" for adverbs.

a Maria was invited to the performance because she is a great dancer. ☐

b The students entered so quietly that I thought they weren't in the room. ☐

c Antonio has to work late tonight. ☐

d I sometimes spend time with my cousins. ☐

e My secretary is a very quick typist. ☐

f There's no reason to be so loud! I'm right here by your side. ☐

7. Notice that many words in English, such as the ones presented in the alternatives below can be tricky to use. It looks like their meanings are the same, but they are not! So, watch out!
The statements below are related to different social communicative situations. They need the appropriate word to complete and create the meaning intended. Choose the correct alternative. Use a dictionary if necessary.

a Mary didn't ______________ the parents' meeting because she didn't receive our invitation by email.

☐ attend ☐ assist

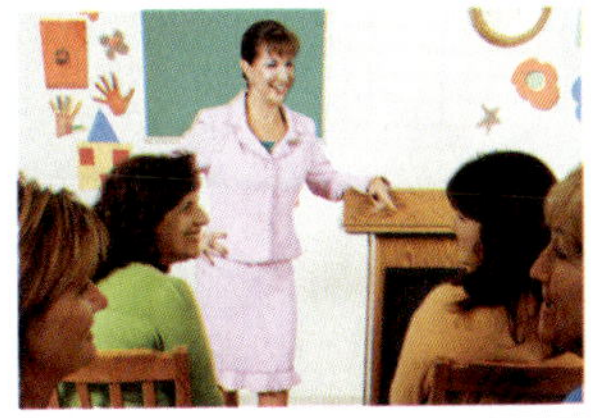
MICHELLE PEDONE/STONE/ GETTY IMAGES

STOCKBYTE/THINKSTOCK

b Do you ______________ to go to a university when you finish high school?

☐ intend ☐ pretend

c The students are ______________ working with false cognates.

☐ actually ☐ currently

PHOTODISC/THINKSTOCK

CREATAS RF/THINKSTOCK

d Mom and dad invited their closest ______________ to their 25th anniversary.

☐ parents ☐ relatives

e Let's take some ______________ math classes before the final test, Paul.

☐ private ☐ particular

COMSTOCK IMAGES/THINKSTOCK

SMART VIEW27/DREAMSTIME.COM

f Our ______________ depends on how much effort we put into the project.

☐ exit ☐ success

✔ Check your answers on page 208.

BERNHARD LANG/RISER/GETTY IMAGES

BEYOND DIGITAL GADGETS

unit 7

NESTA UNIDADE VOCÊ IRÁ:

- usar palavras relacionadas à tecnologia digital;
- identificar as principais características de histórias em quadrinhos;
- usar o verbo *can* para pedir e dar permissão, tratar de habilidades, expressar possibilidades, fazer solicitações;
- narrar ações ocorridas utilizando o *Simple Past*;
- identificar as principais características de comerciais de rádio.

GANDEE VASAN/STONE/GETTY IMAGES

ANNE ACKERMANN/DIGITAL VISION/GETTY IMAGES

- Você reconhece todos os aparelhos mostrados nas fotos? Qual a função deles?
- Você se identifica com alguma das situações nas fotos? Justifique sua resposta.

Have Your Say

1 How important is technology to you?

- ☐ not at all
- ☐ somewhat
- ☐ important
- ☐ very important

2 Match the words to the pictures.

a cell phone
b DVD player
c Smart TV
d tablet
e ultrabook
f video game

3 Rank the gadgets from the previous activity in order of relevance to your life. Show your ranking to a classmate and justify the order.

gadget /ˈɡædʒɪt/ noun [C]
a small piece of equipment that uses new technology

most important

least important

______________________ ______________________
______________________ ______________________
______________________ ______________________
______________________ ______________________

4 Think about the use of the following devices. What do people use them for?

a a computer: to access the Internet, to create documents

b a cell phone:

c a DVD player:

d an MP3 player:

5 Compare your list with your partner's.

6 How can you use these devices to improve your English? Write your ideas.

ROY MEHTA/RISER/GETTY IMAGES

ERTEKMALI/DREAMSTIME.COM

JUPITER IMAGES/COMSTOCK IMAGES/THINKSTOCK

GARY S CHAPMAN/PHOTOGRAPHER'S CHOICE RF/GETTY IMAGES

Reading Beyond the Words

1 Look at the comic strips below and order the panels. Make three different comic strips. Number them 1A–1D, 2A–2C, and 3A–3D.

> **comic strip** /ˈkɒmɪk ˌstrɪp/
> noun a series of drawings that tell a story, especially a funny story

1

1A

2

3

2 Compare your answers to your partners'. Is more than one sequence possible for each comic strip?

3 Read the comic strips on the previous page again and complete the chart.

Comic	Who are the characters?	Where are they?	What is the comic strip about?	What is its purpose?
1		Home.		
2	Five-year-old boy.			To reflect on how habits have changed because of technology.
3			Excessive use of gadgets and their effect on the environment.	

4 Answer the questions below.

a Which character from the first comic strip do you identify with more – the father or the daughter? Why?

____

____

b Why does the boy say "I wonder if people had Google ads on their foreheads back then?"

____

____

c Why are the teens laughing in the third comic strip?

____

____

5 Discuss the questions below.

a Were you able to use a computer when you were a child?

b What (other) devices were you able to use as a child?

c Do you think Internet advertising is effective? Why?

d Can you spend an entire day without using your gadgets?

Genre Analysis

1 Complete the statements about comic strips. Use the words below.

always | rarely | usually

a Comic strips ______________ have dialogues which come in bubbles.

b They ______________ use a lot of linking words.

c They ______________ reproduce oral language.

d They ______________ use visual organization to create the story.

e They are ______________ written in capitals.

2 Match the sound words / expressions to what they represent.

a

c

b

d

Languages

- ◯ laughter
- ◯ typing on a keyboard
- ◯ printing
- ◯ soft typing

3 How are the sounds in the previous activity represented in your country?

a ____

b ____

c ____

d ____

4 Look at the bubbles below. Match the circled resources used in the comic strips to their meanings.

- ☐ same sentence, different speakers
- ☐ no emphasis
- ☐ emphasis
- ☐ same speaker
- ☐ music

Did you know

Letterers are individuals who place word balloons and captions on the finished artwork and fill them with words based on the script.

5 Look at the different speech bubbles and complete the sentences below.

thought bubbles

whispering bubbles

burst bubbles

telepathic bubbles

weak bubbles

a ____________________ are used when a conversation is spoken in a low voice.

b ____________________ are used when someone is shouting.

c ____________________ indicate that the character is speaking telepathically.

d ____________________ show what the character is thinking.

e ____________________ indicate that the character is feeling weak, maybe sick.

Vocabulary

1 Match the icons and areas of the browser tool bar to their names.

address bar | back button | forward button | home button | refresh button | scroll bar | search box

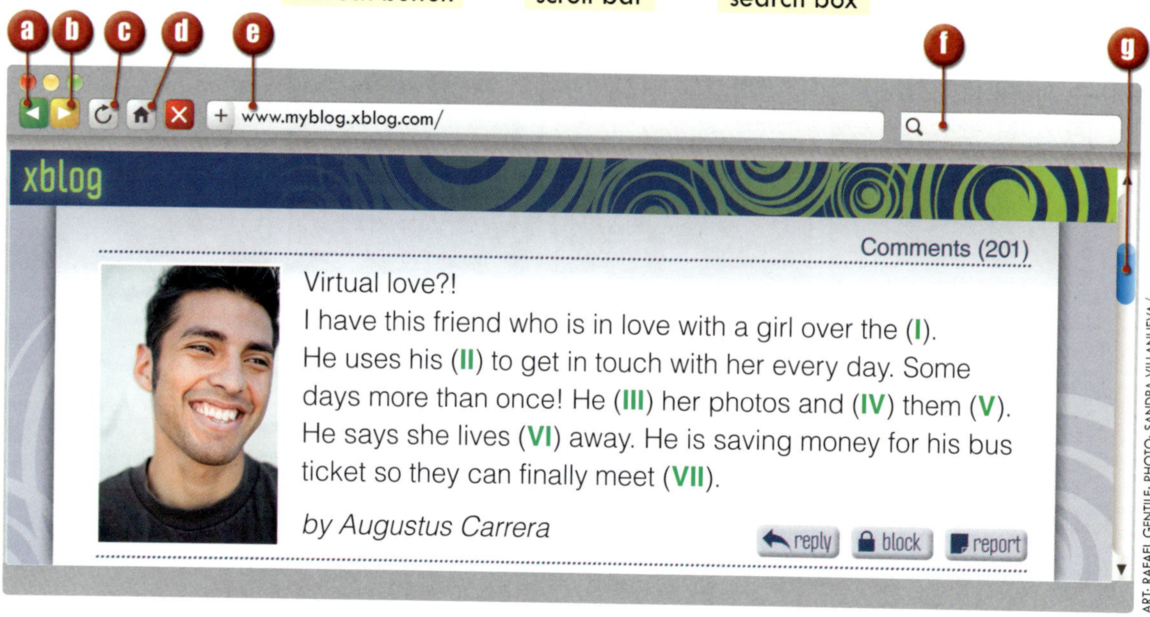

ART: RAFAEL GENTILE; PHOTO: SANDRA VILLANUEVA/ ISTOCKPHOTO/THINKSTOCK

a ______________________ **e** ______________________

b ______________________ **f** ______________________

c ______________________ **g** ______________________

d ______________________

2 Look at the comic strips on page 128 and find words and phrases to complete the blog comment in activity 1.

I Internet **V** ______________________

II ______________________ **VI** ______________________

III ______________________ **VII** ______________________

IV ______________________

3 Unscramble the letters in bold to form words that give meaning to the paragraphs.

a Because young children have access to new technology, their questions about their origins are different now. My three-year-old nephew, for example, (**rodwesn**) ______________ if he was downloaded.

b Gadgets that (**skuc**) ______________ a lot of energy have been called vampire electronics. They consume high amounts of energy because they stay plugged in the (**wohel**) ______________ day and all night too, even when nobody is using them.

Grammar

1 The sentence below is from the first comic strip on page 128. Read it again and choose the correct option to complete the statement.

"Dad, **can I** use the computer for a second?"

In this question, the phrase in bold expresses...

a ☐ ability. **b** ☐ permission. **c** ☐ possibility.

2 Go back to the comic strips on page 128 and copy examples of:

a a question in the Simple Present.

____

b two affirmative sentences in the Simple Present.

____

____

c two affirmative sentences in the Simple Past.

____

____

d one negative sentence in the Simple Past.

____

3 What do you think your parents did or didn't do when they were your age? Complete the sentences below. Look at the pictures if you need help.

a When my mom / dad was my age, he / she had to ____________________.

b When my mom / dad was my age, he / she wasn't allowed to ____________________.

c When my mom / dad was my age, he / she didn't have to ____________________.

d When my mom / dad was my age, he / she needed to ____________________.

In Other Words

Verbo modal: *can*

Os verbos modais são auxiliares, portanto são sempre usados com outros verbos e possuem a mesma forma para todas as pessoas.

Afirmativa		Interrogativa		Negativa	
I	can dance.	Can	I dance?	I	can't / cannot dance.
You			you dance?	You	
He			he dance?	He	
She			she dance?	She	
It			it dance?	It	
We			we dance?	We	
You			you dance?	You	
They			they dance?	They	

RAFAEL GENTILE

O verbo modal *can* pode ser usado para:

- indicar habilidades.

> I **can** type very fast.
> **Can** your grandmother use a computer?

- pedir e dar / negar permissão.

> **Can** I use your computer?
> You **can't** use your cell phones in the classroom.

- expressar possibilidades.

> Technology addiction **can** cause problems.

- fazer solicitações.

> **Can** you follow my blog, please?

Em situações mais formais costuma-se usar a palavra *may* para pedir permissão.

> **May** I use your computer?

Simple Past

No tempo passado, os verbos em inglês podem ser regulares ou irregulares.

"When I **was** your age, I **had** to walk ten miles through the snow to get the Internet!"
I **created** a new profile on the social network I like.

O verbo *to be* no passado tem duas formas.

I, he, she, it	**was**
you, we, they	**were**

Na forma negativa, acrescenta-se a palavra *not* ao verbo.

My father **wasn't** interested in technology.
People **weren't** online 24 hours every day.

Na forma interrogativa, a ordem das palavras na oração é: *was* / *were* + sujeito + complemento.

Were you able to use a computer when you were a child?
Was she late this morning?

Aos verbos regulares, acrescenta-se a terminação *-ed*.

They **discussed** the issue face to face.
It **rained** a lot last week.

As formas interrogativa e negativa são compostas pelo verbo na sua forma básica e o auxiliar *did* (exceto *to be*).

"...they **didn't have** blogging or twitter!"
Did people **walk** around with digital gadgets in the past?

Common time expressions used with the past tense:

- ✔ last (last week / last month / last year)
- ✔ ago (a long time ago / two days ago / one month ago)
- ✔ yesterday
- ✔ the day before yesterday

Practice Makes Perfect

1 Infer the meaning of *can* in the sentences below and match.

1 ability **2** permission **3** possibility **4** request

a OK, class is finished. You can go now. ☐

b You can find news on the latest digital gadgets on my blog. ☐

c Can I see your new tablet? It's so cool! ☐

d This cell phone is too complicated. I can't understand it! ☐

e Peter, can you make a nice presentation for me? ☐

2 Rewrite the sentence that expresses permission using the modal *may*.

____

3 Write an account of Lucas's day using the images below.

Lucas got up at 9 am yesterday, ____

____

____

____

____

____

____

The Way It Sounds

1 Listen to the audio recording and choose the correct answers.

15 **a** What's the number of speakers?

☐ One. ☐ Two. ☐ Three.

b What's the text genre?

☐ Conversation. ☐ Commercial. ☐ Lecture.

2 Listen to the audio again. Check the items that are mentioned.

16

3 What is special about the products?

____

Genre Analysis

These are common characteristics of radio commercials. Check the ones that apply to the commercial you have just listened to.

a ☐ They are short and their messages are clear.

b ☐ Important information is repeated.

c ☐ The announcers speak very slowly.

d ☐ They represent the local culture.

e ☐ They have a specific audience in mind.

TalkActive

Make a radio commercial.

Preparation

- Do you have a cell phone? What are its special features? Check the options below.

- [ ] alarm
- [ ] bluetooth
- [ ] calculator
- [ ] calendar
- [ ] camera
- [ ] clock
- [ ] games
- [ ] GPS
- [ ] Internet connection
- [ ] MP3 player
- [ ] radio
- [ ] SMS
- [ ] TV
- [ ] video player
- [ ] voice recorder
- [ ] others:

____

____

____

____

____

TIP

Use adjectives to emphasize the product, such as *incredible, amazing, indispensable, beautiful*, etc.

- Choose three features you think are the best on your cell phone. Write a short commercial script highlighting these features.

  This incredible cell phone has a 3 mega pixel camera. You can take beautiful pictures and share them with your friends using its fast Internet connection. Get one now! Incredible cell phone with 3 mega pixel camera!

The rehearsal

- Read your script to yourself. Is it clear? Does it repeat the important information?

Sharing

- Present your commercial to the class.

Self-assessment

MAURO SOUZA

AO FINAL DESTA UNIDADE, JÁ SOU CAPAZ DE	
usar palavras relacionadas à tecnologia digital.	
identificar as principais características de *comic strips*.	
usar a palavra *can* para pedir e dar permissão, tratar de habilidades, expressar possibilidades, fazer solicitações.	
narrar ações já ocorridas utilizando o *Simple Past*.	
identificar as principais características de comerciais de rádio.	

Se você deixou de marcar algum dos itens na tabela de autoavaliação, procure no *site* deste livro atividades extras que o ajudem a praticar e consolidar os tópicos desta unidade.

Going Beyond

Song

- "www.nevergetoveryou", by Prozzak. Its lyrics speak of virtual relationships and how real they can be.

Website

- To read more comic strips in English, go to <www.gocomics.com>.

7

Objeto educacional digital

STURTI/E+/GETTY IMAGES

CONSTANT CONNECTIVENESS

NESTA UNIDADE VOCÊ IRÁ:

- aprofundar o estudo sobre *feature articles*;
- entender informações específicas de uma reportagem de TV;
- usar algumas conjunções em inglês;
- estudar as diferentes funções das palavras com *-ing*;
- identificar as principais características de e-mails formais;
- escrever e-mails formais.

HENRIK SORENSEN/RISER/GETTY IMAGES

unit 8

BLEND IMAGES/ARIEL SKELLEY/THE AGENCY COLLECTION/GETTY IMAGES

- De que forma as pessoas estão compartilhando informações nessas imagens?
- Você acha que os aparelhos eletrônicos estão aproximando ou afastando as pessoas das fotos?

Have Your Say

1. Work in groups. Place all the electronic gadgets you have on a desk. Then, answer the questions below.

   a What are the gadgets?

   b What do you use them for?

   c Are they on or off right now?

   d Can you live without them for a day?

2. Who is the most connected person in your group?

3. Is it important for you to be connected all the time? Why (not)?

4. How do you stay connected with your friends? Check all the options you use.

☐ email	☐ SMS
☐ instant message	☐ social networks
☐ online chat	☐ other: ____________

5. When people communicate through email, online chat, instant message, etc., they can use a specific kind of language: Internet lingo. Look at the acronyms, abbreviations, and numbers below and match them to their meanings.

[**abbreviation** /əˌbriːviˈeɪʃ(ə)n/ noun [C] a short form of a word or phrase]

[**acronym** /ˈækrənɪm/ noun [C] an abbreviation consisting of letters that form a word]

a ASAP	☐ before
b B4	☐ best friend forever
c BFF	☐ as soon as possible
d CUL8R	☐ hugs and kisses
e GR8	☐ thanks
f LOL	☐ great
g PLZ	☐ see you later
h THX	☐ laughing out loud
i XOXO	☐ please

6. What are some acronyms and abbreviations you use in your writing? In what situations do you use them?

Reading Beyond the Words

1 What is etiquette? What about job etiquette? Discuss.

2 Read the feature article below and write the subheads in the appropriate space.

Friends and Family at Work — Teen Cell Phone Usage

Teens@Work

Summer Job Etiquette for Teenagers

Job skills teenagers should master before going to work this summer

It is that moment again when teenagers get excited about getting cool summer employment. For many, it will be a first job, and they dream about having their own money for what they plan to buy this summer.

Although teens will definitely learn new job skills on their summer jobs, employers require that teens master certain fundamental summer job etiquette before they arrive at work. Here are a few job etiquette tips for working teens that reduce employer anxiety.

____

Oh the cell phone! Everyone knows how important personal cell phones are to teens. In fact, TeenFrontier.com reports that 25% of cell phone revenues come from teens. Summer job etiquette demands that teenagers control the use of personal cell phones in the workplace. To be considered a professional working teen at a summer job, keep cell phones off, avoid texting and do not wear earphones while working.

____

Whether this is a first summer job or the tenth, having friends and family "visit" an employee at work is not good summer job etiquette. Of course, it is acceptable if teens are working in the food court in the mall and family stops by to buy food. However, teen friends are just not welcome to "hang out" in the food court during the slow times.

Summer is almost here and teenagers should be on their best behavior if they want to work.

4 Teen Drops

ART: RAFAEL GENTILE; PHOTO: MANGOSTOCK/ISTOCKPHOTO/THINKSTOCK

Adapted from <http://voices.yahoo.com>. Accessed on Oct 31, 2012.

3 Read the feature article on page 143 again and check the best options.

a The article is written for:

- ☐ teenagers.
- ☐ parents.
- ☐ employers.

b The objective of the article is to:

- ☐ discuss new ways teenagers can use their cell phones.
- ☐ demonstrate how family and friends can interfere with teen jobs.
- ☐ inform teenagers of proper behavior at work.

c The author of the article believes teenagers:

- ☐ need summer jobs to buy new things.
- ☐ are not aware of employer expectations.
- ☐ visit family and friends too often.

4 Answer the following questions about the feature article on the previous page.

a Why do teens want a summer job?

____

b What do teens have to master before they arrive at work?

____

c What does summer job etiquette demand about the use of cell phones?

____

d In which case is it acceptable to have friends and family visit an employee at work?

____

5 Summarize the content of the article by writing a list of do's and don'ts at work.

Etiquette at work

Do's	Don'ts
keep cell phones off	

RAFAEL GENTILE

6 Discuss the questions below. Justify your opinions.

a Do you think the etiquette rules apply only to summer-job employees or to all kinds of workers?

b Do you think the etiquette rules apply to school as well? Why?

c Besides the examples mentioned in the text, discuss other situations when it is inappropriate to use a cell phone. Use a dictionary if necessary.

Genre Analysis

1 What is a feature article? Complete the paragraph below.

Feature articles are published in ____ ____. They focus on ____________ subjects that interest the audience they are written for.

2 Go back to page 70 and check your answers.

3 Complete the statements below about the elements of feature articles.

body   conclusion   introduction   title

a The ____________ shows originality to attract the readers' attention.

b The ____________ previews why the article will be relevant and interesting.

c The ____________ consists of one or more paragraphs of ideas and arguments and shows a clear division of ideas with use of subheads and bullets.

d The ____________ reviews the main ideas and makes a final point.

4 Read the definitions below and check the options that are used to describe the tone and style of feature articles.

The tone is how the writer shows his / her attitude towards the subject of the text. It may be formal, informal, intimate, playful, serious, ironic, etc.

Based on <classweb.gmu.edu>. Accessed on Feb 18, 2013.

The style is how the writer describes events, objects, and ideas. It influences word choice, sentence structure, figurative language, and sentence arrangement.

Based on <readwritethink.org>. Accessed on Feb 18, 2013.

- [ ] formal language
- [ ] informal language
- [ ] unemotional sentences
- [ ] relevant jargon

Vocabulary

1 The words and expressions below are from the feature article on page 143. Match them to their definitions.

a	avoid	☐	spend time with
b	food court	☐	need
c	hang out	☐	sending text messages
d	require	☐	to choose not to do something
e	revenue	☐	gain, profit
f	texting	☐	group of food stores in a shopping mall with a central area where you can sit at tables and eat your food

2 To avoid repeating words, writers use synonyms. Find synonyms for these words below in the article on page 143.

a master: ______________________ **c** employment: ______________________

b demand: ______________________ **d** stop by: ______________________

3 Read the statements extracted from the article and pay attention to the highlighted words. Look at the example and complete the table by forming new words.

- Here are a few job etiquette tips that reduce employer anxiety.
- Having friends and family "visit" an employee at work is not good summer job etiquette.

Verb	The person who does the action	The person who is affected by the action
employ	*employer*	*employee*
examine		
interview		
train		

4 Use the words or expressions below to complete the following statements.

acceptable avoid hanging out skills

a Reading good books and writing are excellent ways to improve your writing ______________________.

b I just love ______________________ with my family and friends after work and on weekends.

c Surfing the Internet at work is not ______________________ in many companies.

d With all these gadgets around me, how can I ______________________ getting distracted?

Grammar

1 Write the words below in the correct column according to their meaning.

and however if in fact whether

addition	contrast	condition	emphasis
in addition (to)	although	as long as	as a matter of fact
as well as	but	unless	even
too	instead		actually

RAFAEL GENTILE

2 Fill in the blanks using words from the previous activity.

Natural Sciences

________________ you have turned off your computer, microwave, TV, and DVD player, they still use electricity. ______________________, most home electronics continue to consume power when they are in the off mode. __________________ electronic gadgets in standby mode seem to be off, they are not. They consume a small amount of power that adds up over time. These vampire electronics increase your electricity bill ____________________ increase the price of energy in general. ________________ that, they pollute the environment. ________________, you can help save energy by unplugging all electronic devices after using them.

ART: SÉRGIO ONDOERA; PHOTO: STANKO07/DREAMSTIME.COM

3 Study the different uses of *-ing* words in these sentences from the article on page 143. Are they all in the continuous tense?

a It is that moment again when teenagers get excited about getting cool summer employment.

b (...) avoid texting and do not wear earphones while working.

c (...) having friends and family "visit" an employee at work is not good summer job etiquette.

d Of course, it is acceptable if teens are working in the food court in the mall and family stops by to buy food.

In Other Words

Linking words

Linking words são palavras que têm a função de conectar ideias em uma oração ou conectar orações em um texto. As conexões podem indicar várias noções, como:

- adição: and, as well as, besides, etc.
- contraste: although, however, etc.
- motivo: because, since, etc.
- sequência: first, then, next, etc.
- resultado: so, therefore, etc.

-ing forms

Palavras terminadas em *-ing* podem funcionar como:

- adjetivos.

> That subject is really bor**ing**.
> The ris**ing** prices scared her.

- substantivos.

> My favorite hobby is danc**ing**.
> I love swimm**ing**.

- indicadores do gerúndio.

> She **is** writ**ing** an email right now.
> I **was** walk**ing** home when I was mugged.

Em frases, as palavras terminadas em *-ing* podem:

- ter a função de sujeito.

> Learn**ing** German is my goal.
> Play**ing** chess is challenging.

- ter a função de complemento de determinados verbos como *admit*, *avoid*, *consider*, *delay*, *deny*, *enjoy*, *feel like*, *finish*, *forgive*, *involve*, *mind*, *practice*, *suggest*, etc.

> We considered go**ing** to a different school.
> I don't mind do**ing** the dishes.

- funcionar como complemento após determinadas preposições.

> Ligia is really good at play**ing** the guitar.
> I'm really excited about go**ing** to Berlin!

Practice Makes Perfect

1 What idea do the linking words express in the sentences below?

cause | condition | contrast | emphasis

a Silvia bought a new notebook, **even though** she had no money. contrast

b David was late for school **because** he overslept. ____________

c **Instead** of studying for the exams, Mike went to the game. ____________

d **Unless** you tell me your name, I won't be able to help you. ____________

e I can't live without my phone. **In fact**, I have it with me all the time. ____________

2 Complete the sentences with your own ideas.

a I didn't go to the movies. Instead, ____________.

b I always watch ____________. As a matter of fact, I ____________ ____________.

c Although all my friends live in ____________, we never ____________.

d As long as the weather is good this weekend, I ____________.

e Unless you tell me ____________, I ____________.

3 Rewrite the sentences using the linking word in parentheses.

a Although my family and I were out of town last month, my electricity bill was a bit expensive. (however)

My family and I were out of town last month. However, my electricity bill was a bit expensive.

b A friend of mine told me to turn off all equipment before I travel and, after that, unplug them, so they don't waste energy on the stand-by mode. (then)

____

____

c The red light is not a sign of saving energy so the stand-by mode is not very economical. (therefore)

____

____

d Next time I travel, I'll remember to turn off all the electronics and to unplug them too. (as well as)

____

____

4 Circle the correct option.

a Teenagers who are **look** / **looking** for their first job should learn about work etiquette.

b **Answer** / **Answering** the cell phone in public places is extremely rude.

c Since you have the money, you can **buy** / **buying** a new computer.

d He had an accident while he was **text** / **texting** and **drive** / **driving**.

e It's nice to **turn** / **turning** my phone off in class. I don't really like **be** / **being** connected all the time.

f I'm not so good at **text** / **texting**. I can't find the right keys on my cell phone.

5 Complete the sentences with the correct form of the verbs.

a James and his friends are ________________ (plan) their summer vacation.

b ________________ (help) in a restaurant is hard work.

c I'm interested in ________________ (learn) more about your projects.

d Brazil has a zero tolerance law for ________________ (drink) and ________________ (drive).

e ________________ (play) games on the computer is one of my favorite activities to kill time.

f Gabriel's favorite hobby is ________________ (spend) time with his pets.

6 Look at the pictures and write sentences about them using some of the words below and the *-ing* form.

answer | class | disturb | eat | meal | movie | text

PAWEL GAUL/ISTOCKPHOTOS/THINKSTOCK

a Texting while driving can cause accidents.

PURESTOCK/THINKSTOCK

c ________________________________

ISTOCKPHOTO/THINKSTOCK

b ________________________________

PURESTOCK/THINKSTOCK

d ________________________________

The Way It Sounds

TAPULEASA/ISTOCKPHOTO/THINKSTOCK

1 Listen to a TV report. What is the main topic?

17 **a** ☐ Text messages. **b** ☐ Phone calls. **c** ☐ Emails.

2 Listen to the report once more and do the activities below.

18 **a** The report focuses on a group of people who are:

- ☐ entering the job market.
- ☐ in the middle of their careers.
- ☐ leaving the job market.

b Check the topics that are not mentioned in the report.

- ☐ Users are in their teens or twenties.
- ☐ Cell phones must be banned from classrooms.
- ☐ They usually have trouble writing business emails.
- ☐ An email can leave a good or a bad impression.
- ☐ Texting is OK in business situations.

3 What is the main message of this report?

____

____

4 How about your writing skills? Can you adapt your Portuguese language use according to the situation? Discuss.

TalkActive

Discuss email etiquette.

Preparation

- Read the statements below and write A if you agree, U if you are undecided, and D if you disagree with them.
- Write two more sentences about email etiquette.

	You	Your partner
Teenagers are creating a language of their own.		
Teenagers' writing is always conversational.		
It is OK to use acronyms / abbreviations like tks (thanks) in a business email.		
Writing to companies in a casual style can make a bad impression.		
Email etiquette is a skill only teenagers need to develop.		
______________________________________.		
______________________________________.		

The discussion

- Talk to your partner about the sentences in the chart above.
- Take turns and tell each other your opinion about the sentences.
- Use the expressions below to agree, disagree, or agree partially with your partner's opinions.

Expressions to agree	Expressions to disagree	Expressions to agree partially
I totally agree with you.	I don't agree with you.	That's true, but...
I am of the same opinion.	I'm sorry, but I disagree.	It is not as simple as it seems.
That's exactly what I think.	I'm afraid, I can't agree with you.	I agree with you in part, but...

RAFAEL GENTILE

- Try to reach a conclusion about the topics you discussed.

Sharing

- Tell your classmates about your discussion.
- Mention if your opinions were similar or different.
- Finish with the conclusion you reached at the end of the discussion.

Put It in Writing

Plan your writing.

What to write: A formal email.

Purpose: To thank a teacher for his or her help. / To get information about a course in an English-speaking country.

Audience: Your teacher. / The school registration officer.

Emails are used in formal and informal situations. It is important to follow some tips to guarantee your emails are adequate for the situation.

What problems do you find in the email below? Fill in the chart.

From: cuteanne@coldmail.com
To: mrsvalente@schoolmail.com
Subject:

Dear Mrs. Valente.

thank you for being the nicest teacher ever. you're helping me a lot thanks for giving me the chance to be in your class one more time. im a much better std now than i was b4.tks to you!

sincerely.
Anne Davis

SERGIO ONODERA

Problem	Email	Correction / explanation
Address		
Subject		
Capitalization		
Punctuation		
Acronyms/abbreviations		
Level of formality		

Cross out the wrong information in the sentences below. Rewrite them when necessary.

- Avoid having email addresses that are inappropriate for formal contexts.
- In the email subject field, include a long and specific subject.
- Use a proper greeting at the start. Use "Dear" followed by the person's title and name. When you do not know the addressee's name, use "Dear Sir / Madam." If it is addressed to a colleague, you can use "Hi" or "Hello" and the person's last name.
- In the main body, be concise and stick to the subject – say who you are and why you are writing.
- If there is an attachment, do not inform what it is and what needs to be done with it.
- Use a general closing, such as "Best wishes," "Sincerely," "All the best." If your salutation is "Dear Sir / Madam," end the email with "Yours faithfully."
- Do not sign your name.

Choose one of the situations below and write an email about it in your notebook.

Situation 1

Write your English teacher a thank-you email for helping you during the year.

Situation 2

You would like to take a short English course in an English-speaking country. Write to a school asking for information on dates, times, duration of course, and fees.

Use the checklist below to revise your text.

		Yes	No
1	It respects the characteristics of the genre.		
2	It meets my writing objectives.		
3	The language is appropriate to my audience.		
4	The text uses good grammar and punctuation.		

- If you checked *no* in any topic above, rewrite your email.

Exchange your email with a classmate and proofread each other's email. Is it logical? Check grammar, spelling, punctuation, and make comments.

Rewrite your email according to your classmate's suggestions and send it.

Self-assessment

MAURO SOUZA

AO FINAL DESTA UNIDADE, JÁ SOU CAPAZ DE	
entender com mais profundidade um *feature article*.	
compreender informações específicas de uma reportagem de TV.	
usar algumas *linking words*.	
entender as diferentes funções das palavras com *-ing*.	
identificar as características de e-mails formais.	
escrever e-mails formais.	

Se você deixou de marcar algum dos itens na tabela de autoavaliação, procure no *site* deste livro atividades extras que o ajudem a praticar e consolidar os tópicos desta unidade.

Going Beyond

Songs

- "Bug-a-boo," by Destiny's Child: this song has a funny approach to how technology, when used immoderately, can hurt a relationship between two people.
- "Trapped in a Box," by No Doubt: this song criticizes the way some people are overly influenced by "the box," i.e., the TV.

Websites

- <www.emilypost.com/teen-scene>: gives tips about etiquette on different activities in your daily routine.
- <www.kidzworld.com/article/3501-how-to-find-your-first-summer-job>: tips on finding a first summer job.

Objeto educacional digital

Video Producer

What is it like to be a video producer? Read the profile below.

Video Producer Profile

Meg McHutchison
Video Producer / Director
Self-Employed – 15 years in the field

ART: RAFAEL GENTILE; PHOTO: WITHGOD/DREAMSTIME.COM

Read an insider's perspective on video producer careers.

How did you get started as a video producer?

My first job was as a script supervisor. The process of working with a group of people was similar to theater, and I loved it. I found that I was really good at organizing things and people.

What are the main stages of video production?

Pre-production involves scripting or development. People need to agree on the script, the budget, and the schedule. When the creative direction and the budget are approved, then you start organizing the logistics of the crew, securing equipment, locations, etc. In production, you go out and film. You film the pieces, and then put them together. Post-production includes editing, graphics, refining the audio and sound design.

What do you most enjoy about being a video producer?

What's most satisfying is the development process and the editing process. I shoot occasionally, but the creative direction is the most satisfying: writing, figuring out the shots, editing. Video production requires more than one person to make it work, and I work well in creative collaboration.

What is the most challenging aspect of a video producer's job?

Usually the most difficult part is working with clients who don't understand the area or how much money, time, and effort is necessary to complete a product. ■

Adapted from <www.allartschools.com>. Accessed on Nov 9, 2012.

Do you have the key skills to become a video producer? Check YES or NO in the table below.

Can you:	Yes	No
work well in creative collaboration with others?		
create graphics and design digital video effects?		
follow a strict budget and deadline?		
deal with computer hardware and applicable software?		
adapt quickly to changing priorities and projects?		
stay calm in stressful situations?		
conceptualize creative and innovative ideas?		

Would you like to become a video producer? Why?

FACT FILES (part IV)

Writing a fact file

What to write: A cool job fact file.

Purpose: To share information about some jobs.

Audience: Your group or your school community.

Use the information on page 119 to write the final version of your fact file.

A COOL JOB

Description ______________________________

____

____

Benefits ______________________________

____

Work for ______________________________

____

Advantages ______________________________

____

Disadvantages ______________________________

____

Professional options ______________________________

____

RAFAEL GENTILE

Revise your work. Use the checklist below.

	Yes	No
1 It respects the characteristics of the genre.		
2 It meets my writing objectives.		
3 The language is appropriate to my audience.		
4 The text uses good grammar and punctuation.		

✔ If you checked *no* in any topic above, rewrite your fact file.

Share your file with your classmates and read your classmates' files.

Which are the three coolest jobs in your opinion? Why?

SELF-STUDY units 7-8

1. Before reading, it is always a good idea to skim the text. Answer the following questions to yourself: What is the comic strip about? Who created it? Who are the characters? Where does the conversation take place?
Now, analyze the statements that follow and write T (True) or F (False) accordingly.

Extracted from <www.dilbert.com/>. Accessed on Nov 21, 2012.

act up (phrasal verb): começar a apresentar problemas
crash (verb): parar de funcionar
inoculate (verb): vacinar
rebate form: cupom de reembolso
scheme (noun): plano
should (modal verb): dever

a At first, Dilbert is ready to help his mother. ☐

b Dilbert is not sure if his mother really needs all of that help. ☐

c Dilbert's mother wants her son's help because she doesn't know how to use the Internet. ☐

d They have a bad connection and she has to end the conversation, but she hopes he'll help her immediately. ☐

e Dilbert's mother wants him to move back to her house. ☐

f Dilbert's mother pretends she needs her son's help to get what she wants: his giving up on moving back in with her, for at least 6 months. ☐

2. What did Dilbert's mother say she needed help with? Check all the correct alternatives.

a her new webcam plug ☐

b a rebate coupon ☐

c changing her ringtone ☐

d buying a TV ☐

e her laptop ☐

f the telephone connection ☐

3. **Refer back to unit 7 to review the use of *can*.**
Now, let's do some more studying. Complete the statements below with *can* or *can't* to make them meaningful and deliver the right message.

a My cousin ___can draw___ cartoons reasonably well. He took a two-year course to learn how to do it. (draw)

b One of the reasons why many young people ________________ a computer with ease is because they were born in the digital technology era. (use)

c People ________________ on their cell phones on an airplane because they interfere with the terrestrial cellular phone network. (talk)

d Student: ________________ I ________________ the report using my computer? (present)

Teacher: Of course you can. This will surely make your presentation a lot better.

e Being labeled as a digital immigrant doesn't mean a person can't use computers as well as digital natives. People ________________ "new" things at any age and succeed. (learn)

f People ________________ just ________________ old batteries in the trash.
It's recommended that you take them to a local recycling center because there they ________________ these objects with all the necessary care. (put – deal with)

4. **A recount is the act of telling someone about a specific event or life experience that happened in the past. Before doing the activity, read the recount below and answer the following questions to yourself and make notes if necessary: What is it about? Is it told in the first or third person singular? Can you find out who reported this life experience? Why? Why not? Now, complete the recount with the verbs below in the past tense.**

be | drive | get | have | make | send | survive | text | try

Sometimes I wonder how people ____________ in the past without any electronic gadgets. I really can't imagine a world without cell phones, computers, or the Internet! How ____________ people ____________ in touch with each other? ____________ they ____________ letters every day? ____________ they ____________ phone calls through their landlines?

Last month my family and I spent five days on a farm in the countryside and we ____________ any wireless connection or cell phone reception. I almost went crazy! I ____________ texting my friends and it ____________ impossible! It was a very nice farm and there were lots to do, but I still missed being able to interact with my friends online or via SMS. I was so relieved when we ____________ back into the city and I finally got good reception on my cell phone! I ____________ all my friends right away!

5. The use of linking words make your oral speech and your written production more interesting and fluent, that is why it is a good idea to learn how to make appropriate use of them in English. Refer back to pages 147 and 148 to review linking words before you do the following activity.
Complete the statements with the information provided with the images. Use the linking words to connect the two ideas. The first one is done for you.

and | because | but | then | therefore

IMAGESOURCE/MARS

a It wasn't sunny,

but we went to the beach.

___

b Fran can't come tonight

___

___

SHANTELL/ISTOCKPHOTO/THINKSTOCK

STOCKBYTE/THINKSTOCK

c I don't know how to swim;

___

___

d He's bringing the drinks

___

___

JUPITERIMAGES/CREATAS RF/THINKSTOCK

JACKF/DREAMSTIME.COM

e Mix all the ingredients.

___

___

6. Verbs are very important in written or oral texts. Verbs help us understand the meaning of a message. Read the statements below related to different social contexts. They all need a verb in the *-ing* form. Complete them to make meaningful statements. If you need help to review verbs, go back to pages 147 and 148.

cook do learn listen play study talk

a ________________ foreign languages is crucial nowadays.

b Does he enjoy ________________ to music?

c We prefer ________________ the dishes to ________________ lunch.

d Despite ________________ harder than the others, Jane didn't pass her finals.

e Do your homework before ________________ soccer with your friends.

f Anna isn't afraid of ________________ in public.

7. In Unit 7, you talked about digital gadgets. Skim the definitions below. Can you figure out what they are about? Use the context, cognates, and textual clues to write the correct names of the objects.

a A ________________ is a portable data-storage device. It has become the most popular data-storage device among consumers. It has replaced CDs.

b A ________________ is a kind of mobile computer, usually having a touchscreen or pen-enabled interface.

c A ________________ is an oven that cooks food very quickly by passing electricity through it, instead of by heat.

d A ________________ is a telephone that you can carry around with you.

e A ________________ is a camera that takes and stores pictures in the form of electronic signals.

8. Notice that many words in English, such as the ones presented in the activity below can be tricky to use. They look the same, but they have to be used differently.
Test yourself on the appropriacy of the following words. Which one is better for each of the social contexts that follow?

a ________________ (Employers / Employees) give orders to – and pay – ________________ (employers / employees).

b ________________ (Examiners / Examinees) inspect ________________ (examiners / examinees) during tests.

c The ________________ (addresser / addressee) is the sender of a message and the ________________ (addresser / addressee) is the receiver.

d A ________________ (trainee / trainer) is someone who is being trained for a particular profession or job. A ________________ (trainee / trainer) is someone whose job is to train someone.

✔ Check your answers on page 208.

1.

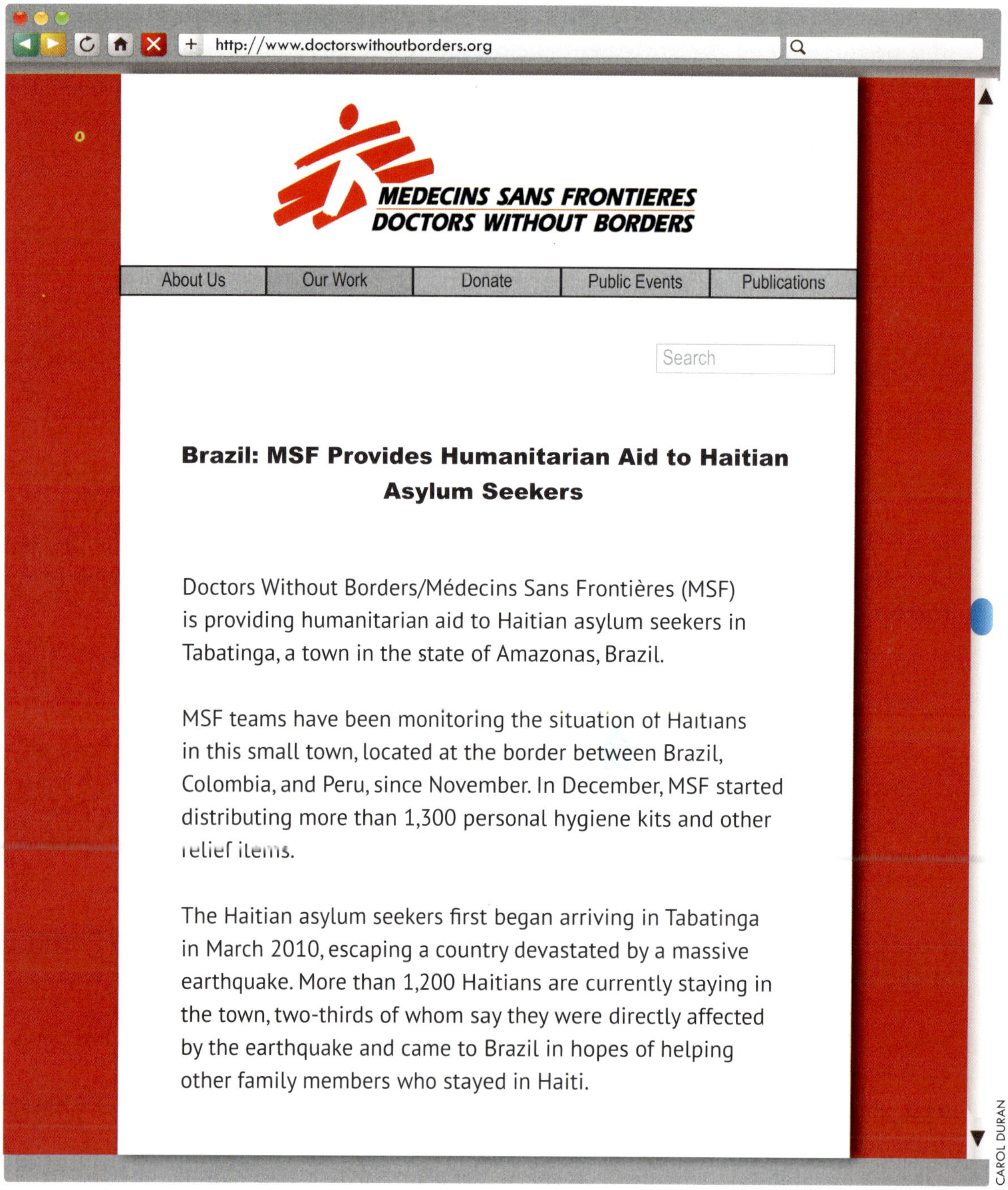

http://www.doctorswithoutborders.org

MEDECINS SANS FRONTIERES
DOCTORS WITHOUT BORDERS

About Us | Our Work | Donate | Public Events | Publications

Search

Brazil: MSF Provides Humanitarian Aid to Haitian Asylum Seekers

Doctors Without Borders/Médecins Sans Frontières (MSF) is providing humanitarian aid to Haitian asylum seekers in Tabatinga, a town in the state of Amazonas, Brazil.

MSF teams have been monitoring the situation of Haitians in this small town, located at the border between Brazil, Colombia, and Peru, since November. In December, MSF started distributing more than 1,300 personal hygiene kits and other relief items.

The Haitian asylum seekers first began arriving in Tabatinga in March 2010, escaping a country devastated by a massive earthquake. More than 1,200 Haitians are currently staying in the town, two-thirds of whom say they were directly affected by the earthquake and came to Brazil in hopes of helping other family members who stayed in Haiti.

CAROL DURAN

Adaptado de <www.doctorswithoutborders.org>. Acesso em 11 out. 2012.

Além de assistência médica, que outro tipo de ajuda pode-se inferir que os asilados haitianos estejam recebendo da organização Médicos Sem Fronteiras?

a ☐ Ajuda a outros membros de suas famílias que ficaram no Haiti.
b ☐ Abrigo, além de livros, kits de higiene e documentação.
c ☐ Ajuda financeira, uma vez que gastaram suas economias na viagem para o Brasil.
d ☐ Gêneros de primeira necessidade, como alimentos e água.
e ☐ Um local para se abrigarem juntamente com outros asilados políticos e desabrigados.

2. 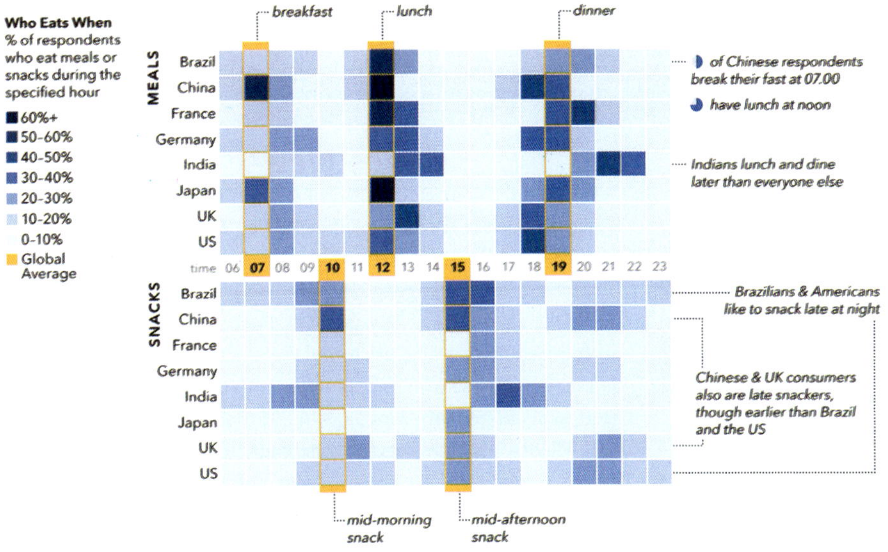

No infográfico acima se tem informação sobre:

- **a** ☐ que horas os orientais e ocidentais preferem fazer suas refeições.
- **b** ☐ a porcentagem de pessoas que comem fora de casa.
- **c** ☐ alguns países onde as pessoas tomam um lanche entre o café da manhã e o almoço.
- **d** ☐ que horas pessoas de diferentes continentes cozinham antes de ir deitar.
- **e** ☐ quais países valorizam a importância de se comer de 3 em 3 horas.

3. 

No cartum acima, a aluna propõe ao senhor Smith um acordo de conduta, informando ao professor sobre sua:

- **a** ☐ forma de aprender, que deve ser respeitada.
- **b** ☐ motivação para começar o ano escolar.
- **c** ☐ preocupação com o conteúdo da disciplina.
- **d** ☐ expectativa de que fará abstrações do conteúdo.
- **e** ☐ confiança de que será bem-sucedida.

4.

http://www.sciencedaily.com

NEWS VIDEO IMAGES BOOKS REFERENCE

Science News

Bilinguals See the World in a Different Way, Study Suggests

Science Daily (Mar. 15, 2011)

Learning a foreign language literally changes the way we see the world, according to new research. Panos Athanasopoulos, of Newcastle University, has found that bilingual speakers think differently to those who only use one language. And you don't need to be fluent in the language to feel the effects — his research showed that it is language use, not proficiency, which makes the difference.

Working with both Japanese and English speakers, he looked at their language use and proficiency, along with the length of time they had been in the country, and matched this against how they perceived the color blue. Color perception is an ideal way of testing bilingual concepts because there is a huge variation between where different languages place boundaries on the color spectrum.

ART: CAROL DURAN; PHOTO: GVICTORIA/DREAMSTIME.COM

Extraído de <www.sciencedaily.com>. Acesso em 8 nov. 2012.

Escolha a alternativa que melhor completa a frase abaixo:
O experimento mencionado no texto utiliza percepção visual para testar os conceitos de falantes bilíngues,

a ☐ já que eles literalmente têm concepções diferentes do mundo.
b ☐ embora eles prefiram pensar nas cores em sua língua nativa.
c ☐ porque eles não precisam ser fluentes na língua a ser testada.
d ☐ contanto que o teste seja feito com a percepção da cor azul.
e ☐ devido à diversidade significativa no espectro de cores entre as línguas.

5.

Na fala acima, fica evidenciado que Calvin:

a ☐ gostaria que seres de outros planetas nos visitassem.
b ☐ admira a força que povos de outras galáxias possuem.
c ☐ se mostra desesperançado com os seres humanos.
d ☐ considera os extraterrestres seres de inteligência mediana.
e ☐ admira pessoas que sabem qual é o seu lugar neste mundo.

6.

+ http://rebekahelle.hubpages.com

search explore sign in join now

Study Habits of Notable Men and Women

1

Albert Einstein's parents encouraged him even though his teachers didn't believe he was that intelligent. He was a true genius and received a Nobel Prize.

2

Sandra Day O'Conner, the first woman Supreme Court Justice, read a lot of newspapers and magazines including *National Geographic, Wall Street Journal*, and the *Saturday Evening Post*. She lived with her grandmother so that she could attend a private school.

3

Martin Luther King, Jr. did so well in class through his reading that he skipped ninth and twelfth grades.

4

Hillary Clinton worked hard during school and was very active in the school government and wrote for the school newspaper. She was vice president of her senior class. Her mother taught her how to remain balanced and to keep her equilibrium even while debating issues.

5

Benjamin Franklin struggled with math, so he made up math games to help raise his grades.

ART: CAROL DURAN; PHOTOS: ALFRED EISENSTAEDT/TIME & LIFE PICTURES/GETTY IMAGES (1); BETTMANN/CORBIS/LATINSTOCK (2); MICHAEL OCHS ARCHIVES/GETTY IMAGES (3); JOEYGIL/DREAMSTIME.COM (4); GEORGIOS/DREAMSTIME.COM (5)

Extraído de <http://rebekahelle.hubpages.com>. Acesso em 12 nov. 2012.

Nos exemplos dados, temos informações sobre pessoas famosas que

a ☐ superaram limites, embora nem sempre tenham se dado bem na escola.
b ☐ apesar de terem se tornado famosos apenas depois de adultos, foram bons alunos na escola.
c ☐ tiveram motivação suficiente para superar problemas com professores e colegas.
d ☐ venceram em suas carreiras, embora tivessem limitações intelectuais comprovadas.
e ☐ souberam usar suas habilidades na escola e no trabalho.

7.

+ www.pbs.org/

HOME | EVOLUTION | NATURE | PLANET EARTH | SEARCH

The Fabric of the Cosmos

The Fabric of the Cosmos, a four-hour series based on the book by renowned physicist and author Brian Greene, takes us to the frontiers of physics to see how scientists are piecing together the most complete picture yet of space, time, and the universe. With each step, audiences will discover that just beneath the surface of our everyday experience lies a world we'd hardly recognize – a startling world far stranger and more wondrous than anyone expected.

Brian Greene is going to let you in on a secret: We've all been deceived. Our perceptions of time and space have led us astray.

Much of what we thought we knew about our universe – that the past has already happened and the future is yet to be, that space is just an empty void, that our universe is the only universe that exists – just might be wrong.

Interweaving provocative theories, experiments, and stories with crystal-clear explanations and imaginative metaphors like those that defined the groundbreaking and highly acclaimed series *The Elegant Universe*, *The Fabric of the Cosmos* aims to be the most compelling, visual, and comprehensive picture of modern physics ever seen on television.

CAROL DURAN

From NOVA, "Fabric of the Cosmos", website (http://www.pbs.org/wgbh/nova/physics/fabric-of-cosmos.html) © 1996-2013 WGBH Educational Foundation

O texto faz um convite para assistirmos a uma série de TV. A abordagem utilizada nos episódios pretende nos convencer de que nossas crenças sobre o universo:

a ☐ estão representadas da forma mais completa e visualmente correta possível.
b ☐ baseiam-se em explicações não simplesmente científicas, mas também metafóricas.
c ☐ podem estar equivocadas e merecem um tratamento desafiador e surpreendente.
d ☐ são baseadas em tudo que já conhecemos e podemos prever sobre o universo.
e ☐ precisam de um enfoque diacrônico, para entendermos de onde viemos e como o universo se formou.

8.

\+ www.canberra.edu.au

ABOUT RESEARCH LIBRARY CONTACTS LOGIN

WORKING IN GROUPS

Group assignments are set to prepare you for your professional future, to give you a chance to tackle significant projects, and to enable you to demonstrate teamwork skills in your CV.

For a group assignment to work well, you will need to:

- → get to know each other;
- → know how to get in contact with each other;
- → make sure that everyone in the team knows what is going on;
- → establish clear goals from the outset;
- → work out your time frame;
- → plan and attend regular group meetings;
- → keep notes of what has been decided;
- → allocate tasks fairly;
- → deal positively and quickly with 'bludgers' (those who do not pull their weight in the group).

ART: CAROL DURAN; PHOTO: GEORGE DOYLE/THINKSTOCK

Extraído de <www.canberra.edu.au>. Acesso em 15 out. 2012.

Segundo o contexto das recomendações acima, qual alternativa seria mais apropriada para ser inserida ali?

a ☐ Digam ao professor qual colega não está contribuindo na realização do trabalho.

b ☐ Elejam os dois melhores alunos para fazer a apresentação final.

c ☐ Escolham pessoas com quem vocês têm desavenças pessoais.

d ☐ Tentem conversar com o(s) colega(s) que se mostra(m) pouco participativo(s).

e ☐ Observem quem escreve melhor para fazer a pesquisa e a redação do trabalho.

9.

When I'm eating in or dining out with friends, someone inevitably pulls out his cellphone to take a picture, send a text, or Google some trivia brought up by the group. (That someone is sometimes me.) When it comes to table manners in our socially connected world, has cellphone usage become acceptable?
It's not uncommon – and even amusing – to see an entire family at a table together, their heads buried in the bright glow of their smartphone screens. I often wonder how we ever survived without our phones to begin with. What's changed in recent years to make us worry about checking every beep and buzz as it comes in, rather than simply savoring a meal and enjoying uninterrupted conversation in person?

DRAGONIMAGES/DREAMSTIME.COM

Extraído de <www.thekitchn.com>. Acesso em 5 mar. 2013.

O autor do texto, ao comentar o uso de smartphones no contexto social:

a ☐ indaga os motivos de não mais aproveitarmos nossas refeições em companhia de outras pessoas.

b ☐ defende a restrição ao uso de celulares em locais públicos como medida educativa.

c ☐ questiona se o uso generalizado desses aparelhos à mesa tornou-se socialmente aceito.

d ☐ também fala de si mesmo, dizendo que sempre usa o celular quando está jantando com amigos.

e ☐ afirma que todos fazemos uso desses aparelhos para tirar fotos, enviar textos ou pesquisar no Google.

10.

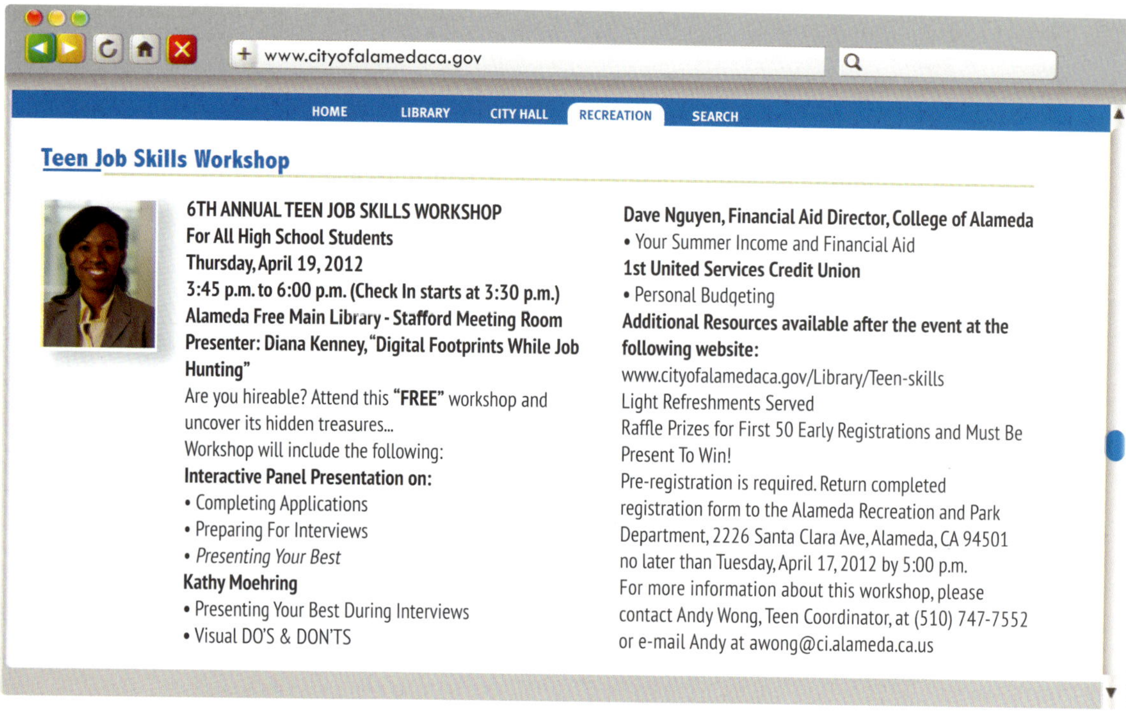

\+ www.cityofalamedaca.gov

HOME | LIBRARY | CITY HALL | RECREATION | SEARCH

Teen Job Skills Workshop

6TH ANNUAL TEEN JOB SKILLS WORKSHOP
For All High School Students
Thursday, April 19, 2012
3:45 p.m. to 6:00 p.m. (Check In starts at 3:30 p.m.)
Alameda Free Main Library - Stafford Meeting Room
Presenter: Diana Kenney, "Digital Footprints While Job Hunting"
Are you hireable? Attend this **"FREE"** workshop and uncover its hidden treasures...
Workshop will include the following:
Interactive Panel Presentation on:
- Completing Applications
- Preparing For Interviews
- *Presenting Your Best*

Kathy Moehring
- Presenting Your Best During Interviews
- Visual DO'S & DON'TS

Dave Nguyen, Financial Aid Director, College of Alameda
- Your Summer Income and Financial Aid

1st United Services Credit Union
- Personal Budgeting

Additional Resources available after the event at the following website:
www.cityofalamedaca.gov/Library/Teen-skills
Light Refreshments Served
Raffle Prizes for First 50 Early Registrations and Must Be Present To Win!
Pre-registration is required. Return completed registration form to the Alameda Recreation and Park Department, 2226 Santa Clara Ave, Alameda, CA 94501 no later than Tuesday, April 17, 2012 by 5:00 p.m.
For more information about this workshop, please contact Andy Wong, Teen Coordinator, at (510) 747-7552 or e-mail Andy at awong@ci.alameda.ca.us

Extraído de <www.cityofalamedaca.gov>. Acesso em 19 out. 2012.

A menção de benefícios como *financial aid* e *raffle prizes* no workshop:

a ☐ mostra o quanto os organizadores se preocupam com os jovens.
b ☐ tem como intuito atrair um maior número de adolescentes.
c ☐ destina-se a alunos de diferentes níveis socioeconômicos.
d ☐ atrai adolescentes de escolas privadas e públicas.
e ☐ atinge alunos com dificuldades econômico-financeiras.

11.

No cartum, o problema do aluno evidencia uma crítica relacionada:

a ☐ à exacerbação do uso dos meios digitais na escola.
b ☐ ao radicalismo conceitual dos trabalhos escolares.
c ☐ ao grau de insatisfação do aluno com os meios que lhe são dados na escola.
d ☐ a uma carência de reflexão crítica na elaboração dos trabalhos escolares.
e ☐ a uma desconsideração das inteligências múltiplas no universo escolar.

12.

ART: CAROL DURAN; FLAG: IBGE

O pôster acima ilustra um fenômeno do mundo contemporâneo. Por meio de um enredo bem-humorado, o leitor pode deduzir que a definição do que significa ser um inglês está representada no texto por uma:

a ☐ listagem de vários estereótipos de conduta de muitas outras culturas.
b ☐ segmentação do texto indicando que o inglês tem atitudes de outras nacionalidades.
c ☐ pluralidade de hábitos do inglês justificada pela tendência à globalização.
d ☐ mixagem de vários tipos de comportamento relacionados com os britânicos.
e ☐ impossibilidade de compreender uma definição apropriada para o “ser inglês”.

13.

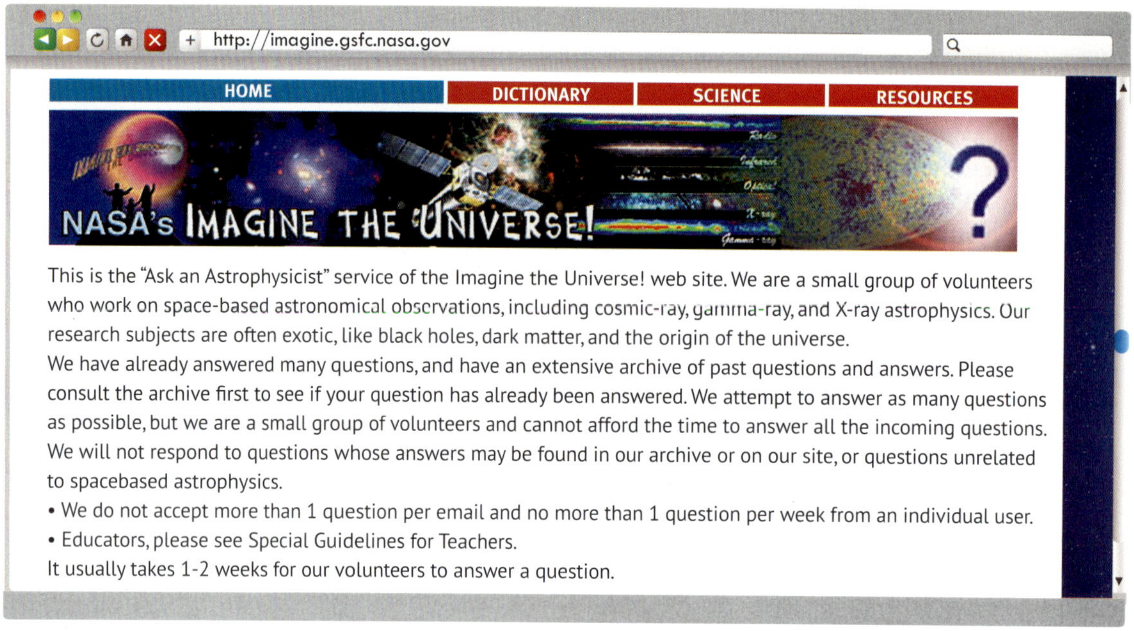
http://imagine.gsfc.nasa.gov

HOME | DICTIONARY | SCIENCE | RESOURCES

NASA's IMAGINE THE UNIVERSE!

This is the "Ask an Astrophysicist" service of the Imagine the Universe! web site. We are a small group of volunteers who work on space-based astronomical observations, including cosmic-ray, gamma-ray, and X-ray astrophysics. Our research subjects are often exotic, like black holes, dark matter, and the origin of the universe.

We have already answered many questions, and have an extensive archive of past questions and answers. Please consult the archive first to see if your question has already been answered. We attempt to answer as many questions as possible, but we are a small group of volunteers and cannot afford the time to answer all the incoming questions. We will not respond to questions whose answers may be found in our archive or on our site, or questions unrelated to spacebased astrophysics.

- We do not accept more than 1 question per email and no more than 1 question per week from an individual user.
- Educators, please see Special Guidelines for Teachers.

It usually takes 1-2 weeks for our volunteers to answer a question.

CAROL DURAN

Extraído de <http://imagine.gsfc.nasa.gov>. Acesso em 19 out. 2012.

A leitura do texto acima nos permite afirmar que se trata de:

a ☐ uma pesquisa para identificar temas de interesse popular em astrofísica.
b ☐ uma chamada para atrair alistamento de voluntários em um *site* de ciências.
c ☐ divulgação de serviço *on-line* destinado a responder curiosidades da astrofísica.
d ☐ um banco de dados relativo a astrofísica, com restrições para temas exóticos.
e ☐ um convite para professores interessados em participar de um projeto científico.

14.

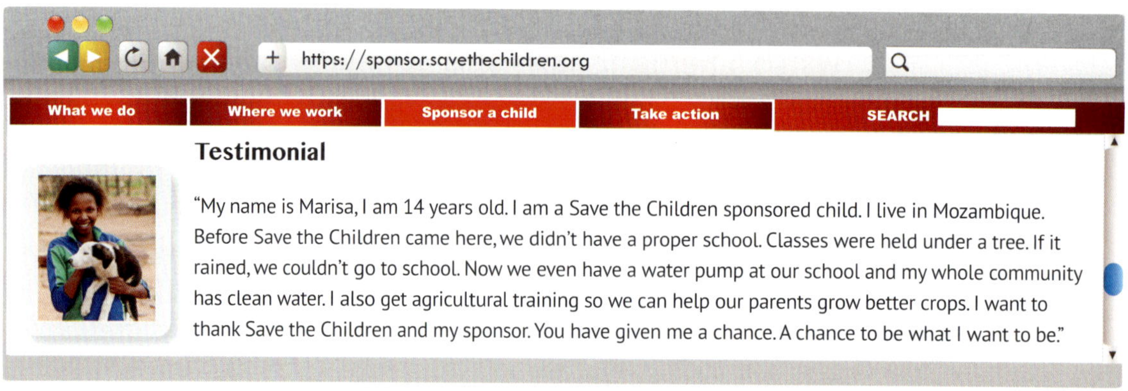
https://sponsor.savethechildren.org

What we do | Where we work | Sponsor a child | Take action | SEARCH

Testimonial

"My name is Marisa, I am 14 years old. I am a Save the Children sponsored child. I live in Mozambique. Before Save the Children came here, we didn't have a proper school. Classes were held under a tree. If it rained, we couldn't go to school. Now we even have a water pump at our school and my whole community has clean water. I also get agricultural training so we can help our parents grow better crops. I want to thank Save the Children and my sponsor. You have given me a chance. A chance to be what I want to be."

ART: CAROL DURAN; PHOTO: ISTOCKPHOTO/THINKSTOCK

Extraído de <https://sponsor.savethechildren.org>. Acesso em 15 out. 2012.

Ao ler o depoimento da garota, tem-se conhecimento:

a ☐ dos dados de quem a patrocina.
b ☐ do local onde ela trabalha.
c ☐ da estrutura do local onde ela mora.
d ☐ de como ela poderá ajudar seus pais.
e ☐ do que ela deseja para seu futuro.

15.

Over 2 million die in developing countries b/c of lack of access to vaccines.

Pneumonia is the single biggest killer of children under 5.

1.3 million children die every year from diarrheal diseases.

There are 1.4 million pregnant women living with HIV.

Children born less than three years apart are less likely to survive & more likely to be malnourished during infancy & childhood through age five.

Malnutrition is associated with 35% of child deaths.

Over 700.000 Malaria deaths in 2009, mainly African children.

3.7 million newborns die in the first 4 weeks of birth each year.

Sources: USAID handout | http://www.unicef.org/aids/index_preventionyoung.html | http://www.child-survival.org/advocacy/2009act.php
http://www.who.int/mediacentre/factsheets/fs094/en/ | Center for Global Development, Education and the Developing World: Why is Education Essential for Development? (2004)

Adaptado de <http://50.usaid.gov>. Acesso em 21 fev. 2012.

De acordo com os dados apresentados no infográfico:

a ☐ a doença responsável pelo maior número de mortes de crianças até cinco anos é a pneumonia.

b ☐ mais de três milhões de crianças morrem até o segundo mês de vida em todo o mundo.

c ☐ a falta de acesso a vacinas provoca a morte de mais de dois milhões de crianças.

d ☐ a malária matou ultimamente quase um milhão de crianças nos países em desenvolvimento.

e ☐ crianças que nascem prematuras têm maiores chances de adquirir doenças que causam diarreia.

16.

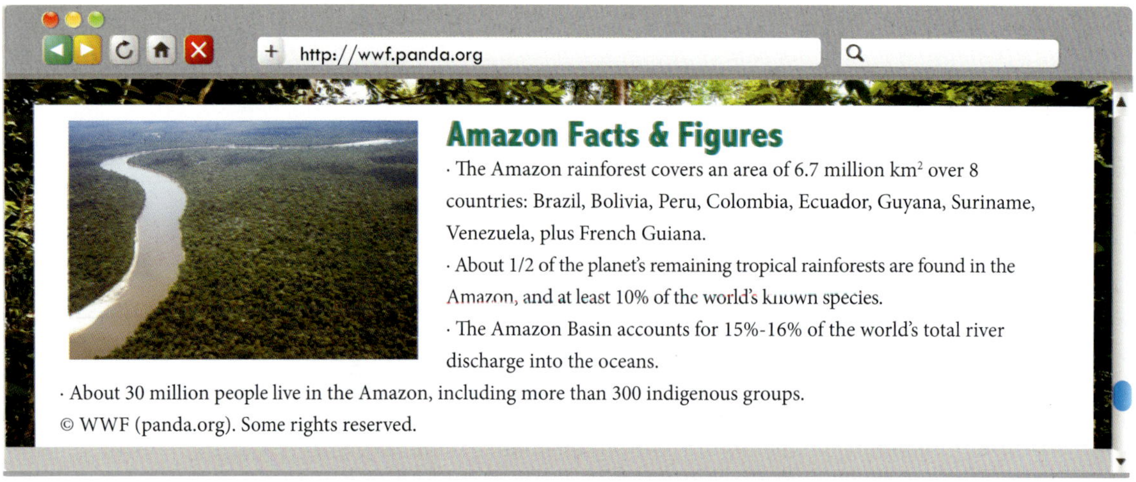

http://wwf.panda.org

Amazon Facts & Figures

· The Amazon rainforest covers an area of 6.7 million km² over 8 countries: Brazil, Bolivia, Peru, Colombia, Ecuador, Guyana, Suriname, Venezuela, plus French Guiana.

· About 1/2 of the planet's remaining tropical rainforests are found in the Amazon, and at least 10% of the world's known species.

· The Amazon Basin accounts for 15%-16% of the world's total river discharge into the oceans.

· About 30 million people live in the Amazon, including more than 300 indigenous groups.

ART: CAROL DURAN; PHOTO: DEB22/DREAMSTIME.COM

Extraído de <wwf.panda.org>. Acesso em 19 out. 2012.

A organização da informação apresentada no texto acima obedece a uma regularidade, que consiste em:

a ☐ apresentar os fatos em ordem decrescente de importância.
b ☐ enumerar os fatores ambientais em detrimento dos fatores humanos.
c ☐ contrapor a extensão da região com a população estimada.
d ☐ anunciar os fatos com informações numéricas ou estatísticas.
e ☐ identificar as ações que a organização WWF considera prioritárias.

17.

AVAILABLE AT <WWW.SHOEBOXBLOG.COM>. ACCESSED ON MAR 10, 20 3.

A expressão "I wish!" se refere ao fato de o coelho:

a ☐ sempre procrastinar suas obrigações quando precisa levantar cedo.
b ☐ viver adiando coisas importantes, exceto seus horários sagrados de tomar café.
c ☐ desejar ter conseguido adiantar um trabalho que deveria ter sido executado.
d ☐ expressar sua vontade de parar de procrastinar a hora de ir para a cama.
e ☐ lastimar quando acaba procrastinando trabalhos que tem que fazer na *web*.

18.

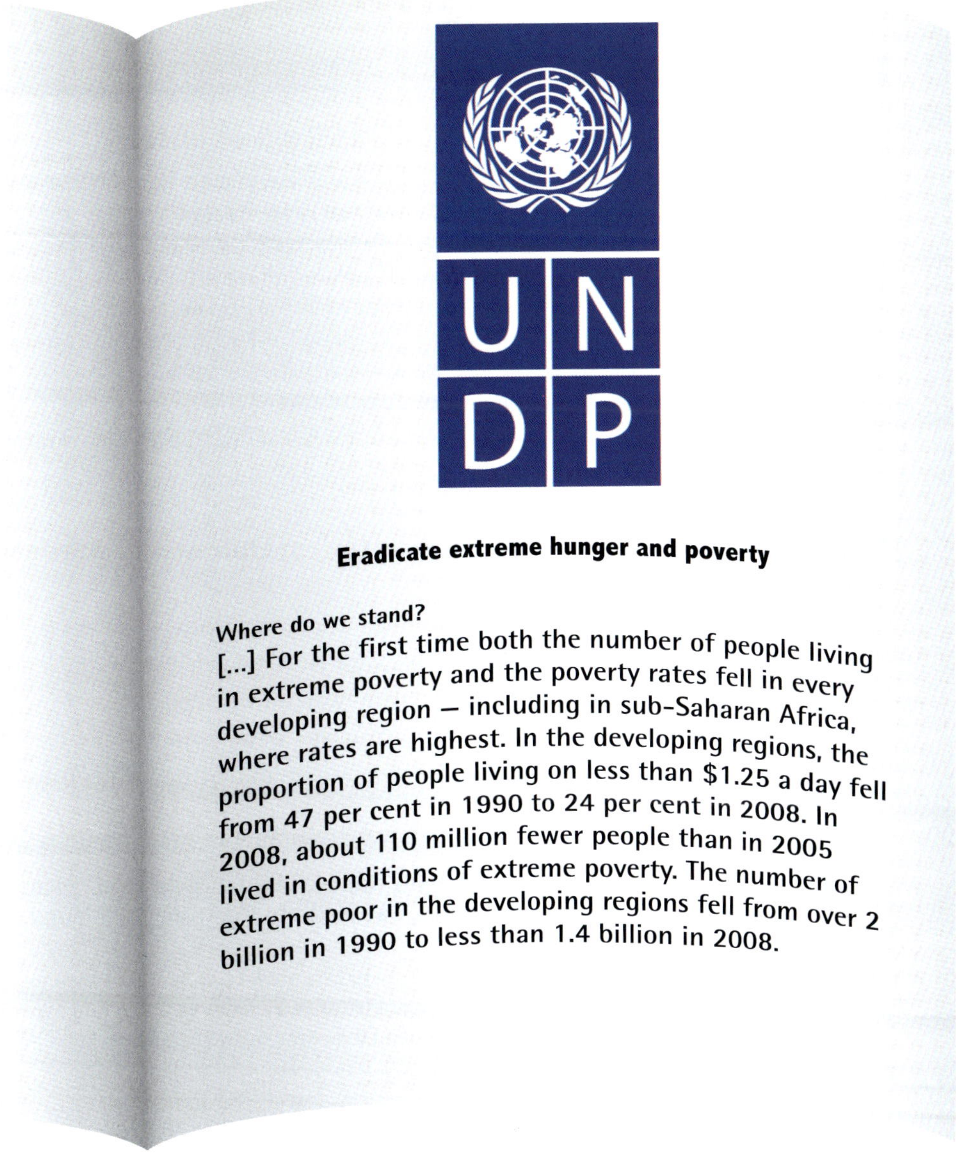

Eradicate extreme hunger and poverty

Where do we stand?

[...] For the first time both the number of people living in extreme poverty and the poverty rates fell in every developing region – including in sub-Saharan Africa, where rates are highest. In the developing regions, the proportion of people living on less than $1.25 a day fell from 47 per cent in 1990 to 24 per cent in 2008. In 2008, about 110 million fewer people than in 2005 lived in conditions of extreme poverty. The number of extreme poor in the developing regions fell from over 2 billion in 1990 to less than 1.4 billion in 2008.

ART: CAROL DURAN; LOGO: UNDP BRAZIL

Extraído de <www.undp.org>. Acesso em 4 mar. 2013.

O texto acima é parte de um relatório da ONU sobre os objetivos de desenvolvimento para o milênio. Tendo-o como base, e considerando que se encontra em extrema pobreza quem vive com menos de $1.25 por dia, podemos afirmar que:

a ☐ mais africanos do Saara encontram-se abaixo da linha de pobreza atualmente, se comparados a outros povos.

b ☐ o número de pessoas pobres que vivem em países desenvolvidos chegava a quase 1 bilhão e meio em 2008.

c ☐ o número de pessoas vivendo na extrema pobreza nas regiões em desenvolvimento caiu praticamente pela metade, em números relativos, em 18 anos.

d ☐ 2 bilhões de pessoas correspondiam a 47 por cento da população mundial em 1990.

e ☐ 600 milhões de pessoas deixaram a extrema pobreza no mundo em 18 anos.

19.

www.upandrunning.blogblogs.com

Up and Running Blog

[...] Reasons you should care about emotional intelligence by Sara Fletcher

In order to run a business in the service industry, you'll need a wide skill set to attract and satisfy customers. A single mistake or lapse in people skills can cause a drastic change, turning your reputation from good to bad. While a variety of factors plays a role in the success of a business, there is one quality that stands out above others – emotional intelligence. If your business is suffering from a lack of individuals with the necessary skills, then focusing on this particular quality can help enhance your chances for success. Emotional intelligence is an emerging factor for workplace success and is defined by the individual's ability to perceive and manage the emotions of oneself and others. More and more businesses are realizing the importance of this skill, and the service industry is no exception.

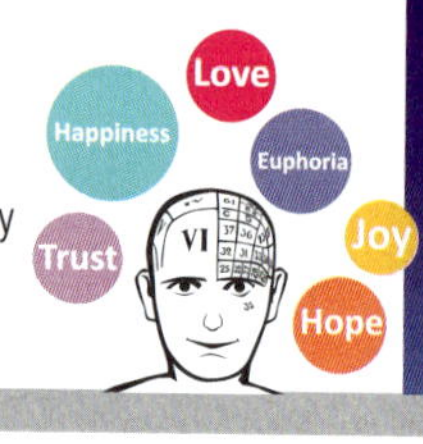

ART: IVAN PRADO; ILLUSTRATION: JIRI FLOGEL/DREAMSTIME.COM

Texto e imagem acima permitem ao leitor concluir que a inteligência emocional:

a ☐ é algo que leva a erros simples, mas pode causar mudanças drásticas nas reputações.
b ☐ sempre foi levada em consideração no setor de serviços, mas não na indústria.
c ☐ está em falta nos indivíduos que circulam no setor de negócios.
d ☐ é o fator preponderante para determinar o sucesso de um negócio.
e ☐ torna alguém capaz de controlar as emoções dos outros e de si próprio.

20.

Time Inc. Study Reveals That "Digital Natives" Switch Between Devices and Platforms Every Two Minutes, Use Media to Regulate Their Mood

According to a new Time Inc. study, consumers who grew up with mobile technology subconsciously move between devices and platforms 27 times per hour and experience fewer emotional highs and lows with media content than previous generations.

(New York, NY) Time Inc., one of the largest branded media companies in the world, commissioned a study titled "A Biometric Day in the Life" to show how the proliferation of digital devices and platforms would affect the media consumption habits of "Digital Natives" (consumers who grew up with mobile technology as part of their everyday lives) and "Digital Immigrants" (who first learned about mobile technology in their adult lives) (...).

CHAD BAKER/THINKSTOCK

Extraído de <www.businesswire.com>. Acesso em 4 mar. 2013.

O conglomerado Time Inc.:

a ☐ realizou um estudo para identificar hábitos de consumo de aparelhos e plataformas, com nativos e imigrantes digitais.
b ☐ precisava diferenciar nativos e imigrantes digitais para direcionar suas campanhas de mídia.
c ☐ constatou que os nativos digitais não se abalam com os conteúdos veiculados pela mídia.
d ☐ conduziu o estudo "A Biometric Day in the Life" para entender, através das plataformas digitais, as mudanças de comportamento entre gerações.
e ☐ quis estudar a influência dos novos aparelhos e plataformas digitais sobre o consumo de mídia das pessoas.

21.

TECHNOLOGY TODAY

Owner wants customers to connect with each other rather than technology

By Sam Shead

A Los Angeles restaurant is offering a deal to customers who agree to look at the person on the opposite side of the table instead of their mobile phone screens.

Eva Restaurant is giving a five per cent discount to customers who are willing to leave their mobile phones with staff when they are seated.

Owner Mark Gold told KPCC radio on Tuesday that the policy is an attempt to create an environment where diners connect to each other instead of technology.

He added that the approach hasn't been implemented to satisfy restaurant-goers that get annoyed by phone chatter or the glow of smartphone screens.

Restaurant staff make the offer to diners when they introduce themselves at the start of the meal.

Gold claims nearly half take advantage of the discount, and many express gratitude at the opportunity to let go of their devices for a while.

Paying attention to your companion during a special meal out might be considered a basic courtesy.

But a survey earlier this year revealed that for 68 per cent of Britons, this is no longer the case, for they would happily take a mobile phone call during a dinner date – even if they know it is not important.

ART: IVAN PRADO; PHOTO: ISTOCKPHOTO/THINKSTOCK

Extraído de <www.dailymail.co.uk>. Acesso em 4 mar. 2013.

Essa notícia sobre um restaurante que oferece descontos aos clientes denota:

a ☐ a preocupação que o dono do estabelecimento tem em relação à privacidade de seus usuários.

b ☐ que mais da metade dos clientes aderiu à ideia e agradeceu pela oportunidade de poder deixar de lado seus equipamentos.

c ☐ o desejo do proprietário de criar um ambiente de conexão entre as pessoas, não mediada pela tecnologia.

d ☐ o incômodo que telas iluminadas e pessoas falando ao celular causam tanto aos clientes quanto aos funcionários.

e ☐ como a ação tornou-se uma oportunidade de marketing para o proprietário, Mark Gold.

22.

How social networks can destroy your social life

An article in the *New York Times* caught my eye. In it, Nick Bilton, a *NYT* columnist, recounts a recent dinner party that he hosted, in the middle of which his phone beeped with a text message. "Hey, I see you're having people over," it read. "OK if I stop by?" What puzzled Mr Bilton was how this person knew he was having a dinner party.

Then he looked at his guests. "Over the course of the three-hour dinner," the poor sap eventually discovered, "my friends posted seven photos on Path, sent six Twitter messages (five with photos), six photos on Instagram and two people checked in on Foursquare. When I added up the collective follower counts of the people in the room, my little dinner party was potentially viewed by more people than watch *The Late Show* on CBS: over three million." (Two of his guests have large numbers of followers on Twitter.) And, to add insult to (self-inflicted) injury, a few days later he telephoned someone in a work-related call, only to be told by the other person – who has never crossed his threshold – how much he "just loved" the lamps hanging above the Bilton kitchen table.

ART: IVAN TOLEDO PRADO; PHOTOS: THOMAS NORTHCUT/LIFESIZE/THINKSTOCK; NAVNIT9/DREAMSTIME.COM; THOMAS NORTHCUT/LIFESIZE/THINKSTOCK; DALLASEVENTSINC/DREAMSTIME.COM

Entre os fatos apresentados no texto acima, um dos mais surpreendentes para o anfitrião do jantar foi:

- **a** ☐ o amigo que se convidou para o jantar através de redes sociais e acabou comparecendo em pessoa.
- **b** ☐ o número de fotos que postaram após a reunião, via Path, Tweeter e Instagram.
- **c** ☐ a quantidade de pessoas que fizeram comentários sobre sua festa, chegando a 3 milhões de *posts*.
- **d** ☐ o comentário feito dias após o jantar por alguém que nunca fora a sua casa a respeito das lâmpadas de sua cozinha.
- **e** ☐ saber que seus convidados bisbilhotaram seus aposentos e postaram comentários em redes sociais durante o jantar.

O texto abaixo é base para as questões 23 e 24.

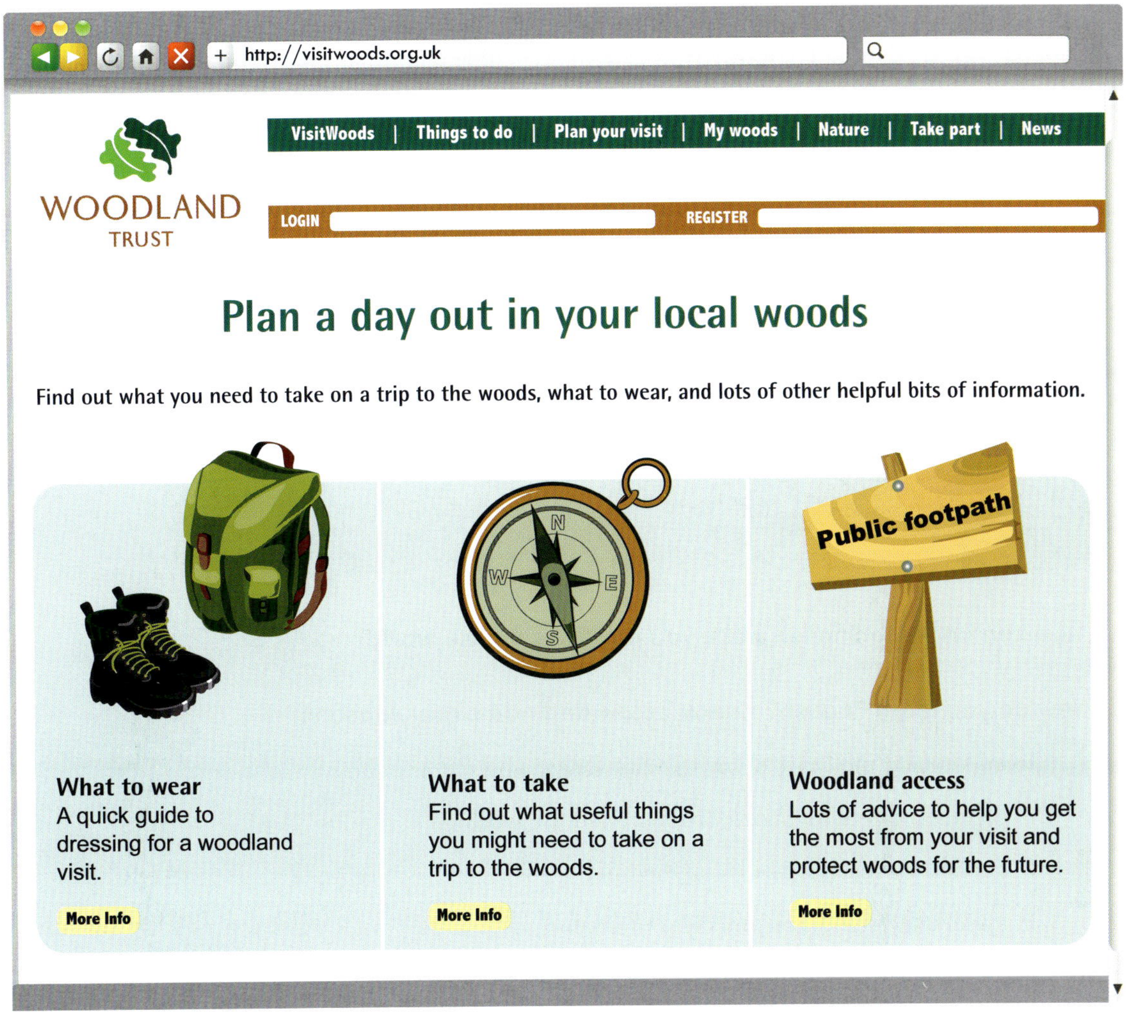

ART: CAROL DURAN; ILLUSTRATION: ISTOCKPHOTO/THINKSTOCK

Extraído de <http://visitwoods.org.uk>. Acesso em 5 mar. 2013.

23. O leitor-alvo do *site* acima seria, supostamente, alguém:

a ☐ interessado em se aventurar por áreas inóspitas.
b ☐ disposto a viajar para conhecer "Woodland", no Reino Unido.
c ☐ consumidor de vestuário típico para acampamentos.
d ☐ engajado nos movimentos ambientalistas.
e ☐ motivado a passear pelos bosques no interior da Inglaterra.

24. O internauta que visitasse o *site* não obteria:

a ☐ informações sobre procedimentos para a preservação do meio ambiente.
b ☐ conhecimento sobre itens de vestuário que não podem faltar em uma caminhada na mata.
c ☐ um guia de compras de utensílios e vestuário da marca Woodland.
d ☐ conselhos para aproveitar ao máximo uma aventura a pé.
e ☐ informações sobre como suprir necessidades em determinada atividade.

Are you a citizen of the world?

MARIO RAGMA/HEMERA/THINKSTOCK

1. How can knowing English make you a citizen of the world?

2. Why do you learn English? Check below and add other reasons.

- [ ] To understand the lyrics of my favorite songs.
- [ ] To communicate with people from around the world.
- [ ] To get better research results on the Internet.
- [ ] To understand stand-up comedians in English.
- [ ] To read comic strips and cartoons in English.
- [ ] To understand what actors say in English.
- [ ] To study in English-speaking countries.
- [ ] ______________________________
- [ ] ______________________________

3. Read the list below. Do you agree with the items in this list? Why?

- **Get access to knowledge:**

Most pages on the Internet are in English.
English is the key to personal and professional improvement.

- **Communicate with people:**

English is the world language of communication. English is everywhere.
Almost all international competitions are conducted in English (e.g. the Olympics).

- **English is easy to learn:**

Simple alphabet. Easy plurals.
Short words. Long words are shortened (e.g. "info" for information).

4. Let's conduct a school survey about the importance of learning English. Follow the steps below. If you have the chance, create your form online and publish it on the Internet.

survey /ˈsɜrˌveɪ/ noun [C] a set of questions that you ask a large number of people about a specific subject

✔ **Step 1: Compose your survey.**

Give it a title.

Create questions. Choose from the options below:

- Wh- questions (e.g. How often do you study English outside of the classroom?)
- Yes / No questions (e.g. Is English your favorite subject?)
- Multiple-choice options (e.g. [ ] once a week, [ ] three times a week, [ ] always)
- Check box options (e.g. Why do you want to learn English? Check more than one option.)
- Scales (e.g. On a scale from 1 to 10, which number best describes your interest in learning English through music?)

✔ **Step 2: Apply your survey.**

Ask the questions to your classmates. Check their answers.

✔ **Step 3: Organize the results.**

Create graphs to represent the results. If possible, go online and use <www.chartgo.com> to make your graphs.

✔ **Step 4: Publish your survey results.**

Post the graphs on the walls of your classroom.

5. Read other classmate's graphs and analyze them. What do the results tell you about you and your classmates? Are you citizens of the world?

A Brazilian in New York

1. In your opinion, what's the stereotype of the English people?

> **stereotype** /ˈsteriəˌtaɪp/ noun [C] a very firm and simple idea about what a particular type of person or thing is like

2. Read the excerpt below and check if the lyrics match your answers in activity 1.

Englishman in New York(by Sting)
I don't drink coffee I take tea my dear
I like my toast done one side
And you can hear it in my accent when I talk
I'm an Englishman in New York
See me walking down Fifth Avenue*
A walking cane here at my side
I take it everywhere I walk
I'm an Englishman in New York

(Chorus)
I'm an alien, I'm a legal alien
I'm an Englishman in New York
I'm an alien, I'm a legal alien
I'm an Englishman in New York
[...]
(* Fifth Avenue is a very famous avenue in New York.)

ART: SERGIO ONODERA; PHOTO LARRY BUSACCA/GETTY IMAGES

Gordon Sumner (Sting). ...Nothing Like The Sun. © Emi Songs do Brasil Edições Musicais LTDA. 1987. Available on <http://www.sting.com>. Accessed on May 13, 2014.

3. According to the excerpt above, what is true about an Englishman?

- [ ] He drinks tea.
- [ ] He doesn't eat toast.
- [ ] He eats toast done on one side.
- [ ] He carries a walking cane.
- [ ] He walks with a guide dog.

4. According to the lyrics, why is the man an alien in New York?

- [ ] He doesn't feel welcome there.
- [ ] He doesn't like the excitement there.
- [ ] He doesn't feel he belongs there.
- [ ] He doesn't like people who live there.

5. In your opinion, what's the stereotype of Brazilian people?

____

____

____

6. Follow the steps below and create a parody.

parody /ˈpærədi/ noun [C/U] a literary or musical work that copies a serious work in a humorous way

Step 1

Review the definition and examples of stereotypes in Unit 2.

Step 2

19 Listen to an extract of Sting's "Englishman in New York" and follow its rhythm by tapping your hands on your desk to the beat.

Step 3

Create a parody with the title "A Brazilian in New York" using your ideas from activity 5. Remember: Humor is a key element in a parody, so it needs to make people laugh! Read an example below.

Original

I don't drink coffee
I take tea my dear
I like my toast done
on one side...

Parody

I have bread and butter
with my coffee my dear
I like to spread butter
on both sides...

ATTILIO

Step 4

Join the lyrics and the melody. If possible, record your parody.

Step 5

Play or perform your parody to your classmates. Is your parody similar to the ones your classmates created?

Celebrate Earth!

1. Read the tips below and add two items to each category.

TIP
When giving tips, use the imperative.

Tips About the Three R's

REUSE

- Use empty jars to store leftovers in the refrigerator.
- Use cardboard boxes to store winter clothes in the closet.
- ____________________
- ____________________

REDUCE

- Take your own bag when you go shopping.
- Turn off your computer when it's not in use.
- ____________________
- ____________________

RECYCLE

- Don't throw away anything that can be recycled: metal, paper, glass, etc.
- Take plastic bottles, old cell phones, and batteries to local recycling sites.
- ____________________
- ____________________

ART: SELECT; ILLUSTRATION: CHRISTOPHER STEER/ISTOCEPHOTO/THINKSTOCK

2. Let's create a project to "celebrate Earth." Follow the steps.

ALEXANDER KALINA/ISTOCKPHOTO/THINKSTOCK

✔ **Step 1**

Choose a week in the next two months to raise awareness about the environment in your school.

✔ **Step 2**

Use some of the ideas from the website <www.earthshare.org> and your tips from activity 1 to make posters and spread them around the school.

✔ **Step 3**

Get inspired by singer Jack Johnson's projects about the environment: <http://jackjohnsonmusic.com>.

JORDI VIDAL/REDFERNS/GETTY IMAGES

✔ **Step 4**

Make a list of all the activities you can do at school to celebrate Earth (e.g. bring an ecologist to talk to students).

STEPHEN MORRIS/ISTOCKPHOTO/THINKSTOCK

- ______
- ______
- ______
- ______
- ______

✔ **Step 5**

Make a list of all the activities you can do around the school to celebrate Earth (e.g. plant trees near the school building).

- ______
- ______
- ______
- ______

PHOTODISC/MARS

✔ **Step 6**

Talk to classmates and teachers and ask for their contributions and ideas.

✔ **Step 7**

Have a green week to celebrate Earth in your school. Suggest the school include "green week" in the annual calendar of activities.

Make a change!

1. **Read the testimonials that answer the question: How would you change the world? Then match the words below to their meanings.**

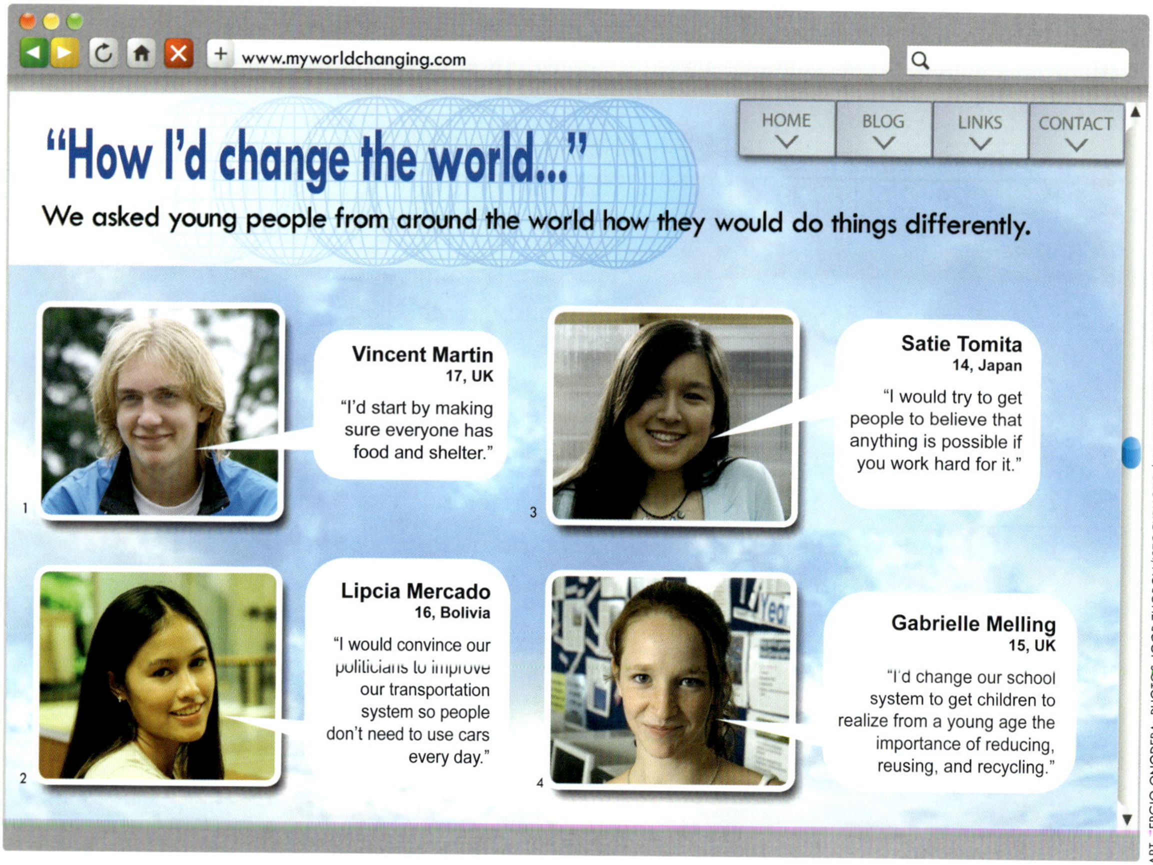

ART: SERGIO ONODERA; PHOTOS: IGOR ZHOROV/ISTOCKPHOTO/THINKSTOCK (1); STOCKBYTE/THINKSTOCK (2); COMSTOCK IMAGES/THINKSTOCK (3); ABLEIMAGES/THINKSTOCK (4)

a make sure	☐	a place where people are protected from bad weather or from danger
b shelter	☐	to know and understand something
c improve	☐	to take the action necessary to be certain that something will happen or be done
d realize	☐	to make something better

2. **Read the quotations again and answer the questions below.**

a Where are the people who gave those answers from?

____

b Do you think there is a connection between the testimonial and the nationality of their authors? Why?

____

c The testimonials suggest solutions for problems people notice in their everyday life. Are those solutions applicable to the problems you notice in your community in Brazil? Justify your answer.

____

____

3. According to Satie Tomita, "anything is possible if you work hard for it." Do you agree with her? Justify your answer.

4. Make a list of the people, projects, programs, or institutions in your community whose aim is to help change or improve people's lives. What do they do?

5. Write your own idea on how you would change the world. Follow the steps below.

- **Step 1**
  Think of an idea you have to change the world.
- **Step 2**
  Write some key words that can help you explain your idea.
- **Step 3**
  Choose one of the ideas presented on the previous page and use it as a reference.
- **Step 4**
  Write down your testimonial. Use the space below.
- **Step 5**
  Share your testimonial with your classmates.

How I'd change the world...

ROBERTA BENITES

Making the right sounds.

1. Use your linguistic and musical intelligences to improve your pronunciation in English. Listen to the pronunciation of the plural words below and check /s/ or /z/ according to the final sounds you hear.

20

a projects ☐ /s/ ☐ /z/
b groups ☐ /s/ ☐ /z/
c diagrams ☐ /s/ ☐ /z/
d colors ☐ /s/ ☐ /z/
e movies ☐ /s/ ☐ /z/
f books ☐ /s/ ☐ /z/
g maps ☐ /s/ ☐ /z/
h puzzles ☐ /s/ ☐ /z/
i animals ☐ /s/ ☐ /z/

TIP
Sounds are represented between slashes //.

2. Underline the plural nouns in the tips below. Then practice their correct pronunciation.

ART: CAROL DURAN; PHOTO: TONGRO IMAGE STOCK RF/THINKSTOCK

Some tips for improving your pronunciation: listen to your favorite artists and groups. Their songs help you become familiar with English sounds. You can also watch TV shows and movies – remember to focus on your listening instead of simply reading the subtitles! And remember, there are many different accents, so keep your choices varied. Listen to podcasts from various English-speaking countries to learn different ways to pronounce the English language sounds.

instead /ɪn'sted/ adv used for saying that one person, thing, or action replaces another

3. Pay attention to the pronunciation of the following plural words. What sound do you hear?

21

boxes glasses wishes kisses roses houses oranges

☐ /s/ ☐ /iz/ ☐ /z/

4. Try reading the following tongue twisters. Choose two of them and practice saying them. If possible, record your voice to help you practice.

tongue twister /tʌŋ ˈtwɪstər/ noun [C] a word or phrase that is difficult to say because it contains many difficult sounds, especially ones that are very similar

A big black bug bit a big black dog on his big black nose.

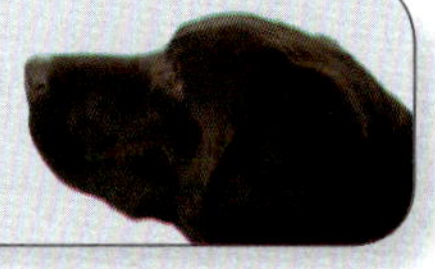

She sells sea shells by the seashore.

Peter Piper picked a peck of pickled peppers.

How much wood would a woodchuck chuck if a woodchuck could chuck wood?

The butter Betty Botter bought was a bit bitter.

A big black bug bit a big black bear, made the big black bear bleed blood.

I can think of six thin things, but I can't think of six thick things too.

5. Say your tongue twisters to your classmates. Try repeating your classmates' tongue twisters.

A bilingual environment

1. What are some characteristics of good learning environments? Check all that apply.

- [ ] chaotic
- [ ] comfortable
- [ ] dark
- [ ] distraction-free
- [ ] noisy
- [ ] quiet
- [ ] well-ventilated

2. Read the following tips on language learning. Then underline the strategies you already use.

www.studygs.net

Study Guides

An educational public service helping learners succeed since 1996: over 10.4 million visitors in 39 languages in 2011. Study Guides and Strategies

HOME | ABOUT | BOOKMARK SGS | SEARCH | TRANSLATIONS&SITE MAP | RESEARCH/AUTHOR | CONTACT

Environment

- **Immersion!**
  Think of creating an environment in your room where you can be in contact with your language.
- **Visit centers and organizations that cater to foreign nationals and immigrants.**
  International student centers, neighborhood and education centers, language and bilingual associations, national halls, consular offices, libraries, etc.
- **Study daily—develop a foreign language habit.**
  Think of studying as you would for a sport or music: a series of skills that need practice!
- **Don't miss a class!**
  And get to know at least one other student to study with.
- **Risk! Be fearless in making mistakes, and getting correction.**
  Would an athlete object when his or her coach corrected certain moves?
  In the same way, this is the role of a language teacher!
- **Think of building your skill set.**
  Basics lead to more complicated variations: for example, use "old" vocabulary to practice new grammar.
- **Study with a friend, in a group, involving yourself in speaking and listening.**
  Play a game online or in the group in the language.

Relax and enjoy yourself!
Do not worry about what you cannot remember, or cannot yet understand, or cannot yet say. You are learning and improving. The language will gradually become clearer in your brain as new connections are made, but this will happen on a schedule that you cannot control. So sit back and enjoy. Just make sure you spend enough time with the language. That is the greatest guarantee of success.

SERGIO ONODERA

Adapted from <www.studygs.net>. Accessed on Nov 12, 2012.

3. How can a bilingual environment help you learn languages?

____

4. Is your school a bilingual environment? Look around and answer the questions below.

a Write down the signs you see in your school. Are any of these signs bilingual?

____

____

____

____

b What other signs would you like to see in your school?

[ ] 

NO RUNNING ON THE STAIRS

[ ] 

NO CELL PHONES IN THE CLASSROOM

CAROL DURAN

5. Let's create some bilingual signs. Follow the steps below.

- ✔ **Step 1:** Use your answers in activity 4 to create different types of bilingual signs to post around the school.
- ✔ **Step 2:** Write your signs on colored paper. Use different fonts and sign shapes.
- ✔ **Step 3:** Share your signs with your classmates. Ask for their opinions on how you can improve your signs.
- ✔ **Step 4:** Ask for the principal's authorization and spread your bilingual signs around the classroom and the school.

REMEMBER: The social communicative functions of posters are:

- to communicate information quickly and efficiently;
- to announce, publicize, or advertise something;
- to grab the attention of the target audience;
- to convey information in verbal and visual ways;
- to carry a simple and convincing message.

Analyzing comic strips.

1. Read the comic strip below. What electronic devices can you see? How useful are they?

____

____

____

2. Which characteristics listed on pages 130 / 131 can you find in this strip? Are there any differences?

____

____

3. Now read the comic strip again and answer the questions below.

a The young man in the cartoon is Jeremy. Who is the couple?

☐ His roommates. ☐ His parents.

Observe the pictures, the characters' posture, and their age.

b Where are they?

☐ At the movie theater. ☐ At their home.

Look at the pictures. What does the place look like?

c Who is the boy talking to in the beginning of the story?

☐ To a friend. ☐ To his mother.

Use your previous knowledge. How do boys talk to different people? Think of choice of words, level of formality, etc.

d Why is the couple annoyed in the last panel?

☐ The boy woke them up. ☐ It was time to get up.

Not all the answers are explicit in the text. You may need to make inferences.

e What do you think about the boy's manners? Are they good or bad? Discuss.

4. Analyzing comics is a good way to learn a language, as they use daily vocabulary and expressions in a natural way. Follow the steps below and practice analyzing comic strips.

- ✔ **Step 1:** Choose a comic strip in English. Print it or cut it out and glue it here. If you prefer to create your own comic strip, you can use <www.toondoo.com> or another website to help you do that.

- ✔ **Step 2:** Now prepare four questions about the comic strip. Look back at the *wh-* words in Unit 2 and ask your teacher for help if necessary.
- ✔ **Step 3:** For each question you ask, create four alternatives, but only one of them should be correct.

1 ______________________________

☐ ______________ ☐ ______________
☐ ______________ ☐ ______________

2 ______________________________

☐ ______________ ☐ ______________
☐ ______________ ☐ ______________

3 ______________________________

☐ ______________ ☐ ______________
☐ ______________ ☐ ______________

4 ______________________________

☐ ______________ ☐ ______________
☐ ______________ ☐ ______________

- ✔ **Step 4:** Ask a classmate to answer your questions.
- ✔ **Step 5:** Answer your classmates' questions. What strategies did you use?

Tech inventions

1. Are digital products a popular gift? Listen to a newscast and find out. (22)

____

2. Listen to the newscast again and write the percentage of people who would like to get each of these digital products as gifts. (23)

ART: SERGIO ONODERA; PHOTOS: OLEKSIY MARK/STOCKPHOTO/THINKSTOCK (1); SVANHORN4245/DREAMSTIME.COM (2); FARZIN SALIMI/HEMERA/THINKSTOCK (3); MAXXREPORY/DREAMSTIME.COM (4); VASABI/ISTOCKPHOTO/THINKSTOCK (5); COBALT88/DREAMSTIME.COM (6)

3. Answer the following questions about smartphone apps.

app /æp/ noun [C] (short for application) a piece of software that is designed to do a particular job, especially one that people use on a smartphone

a Do you use apps? If so, which ones? What do you like about them?

____

____

b If not, which ones do you know? Which ones would you like to have and why?

____

____

c Some people can't imagine life without apps. Others say it's better to experience real life, without apps. Do you agree with one of these opinions? Why? If you don't agree with them, what is your opinion about apps in our lives?

____

____

4. **Read about some fitness apps and match them to their reviews below.**

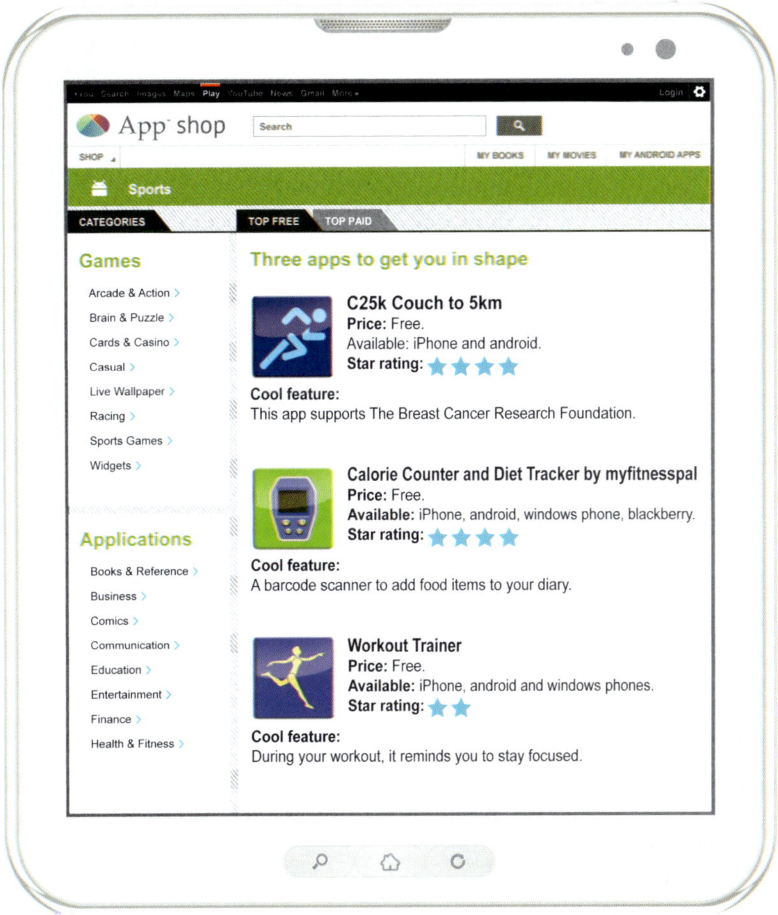

SERGIO ONODERA

TIP

When you read, you always make use of your previous knowledge. Without using what you already know, it's impossible to understand texts.

1 C25k Couch to 5km **2** Calorie Counter and Diet Tracker **3** Workout Trainer

☐ This is one of the best. The sign up process is complicated, but it is worth it as this app has the largest food database of any calorie counter. The food diary lets you record your food intake and track your weight loss. It also provides a daily progress report.

☐ This is a very interesting app. It's a virtual personal trainer with step-by-step audio and visual guides. Instructions and technique tips are really good.

☐ This app may be just what you need to start your exercise routine. It helps you slowly build up from not running at all to 5 km. It lets you know when to warm up, walk, and run.

Based on <www.news.com.au>. Accessed on Nov 26, 2012.

5. **Which of the three apps above would you download to your cell phone? Why?**

____

____

____

GLOSSARY

Aqui você poderá construir seu próprio glossário, com as palavras escolhidas por você ao longo das unidades de seu livro. Inclua nele as palavras novas, aquelas que considera difíceis ou aquelas que quer aprender por alguma razão especial. Você poderá organizá-las em ordem alfabética ou por assunto. Ao incluir uma nova palavra, ponha também sua transcrição fonética entre barras e sua classe gramatical. Essas informações podem ser encontradas em um dicionário. Por fim, acrescente sua definição ou um sinônimo. Caso julgue adequado, poderá incluir, ainda, um antônimo e exemplos de uso da palavra em contextos que sejam significativos. Isso, sem dúvida, vai ajudá-lo(a) a fazer relações com outros conceitos já presentes em sua memória e, assim, você terá maior facilidade de se recordar da palavra e saber como usá-la em diversas situações.

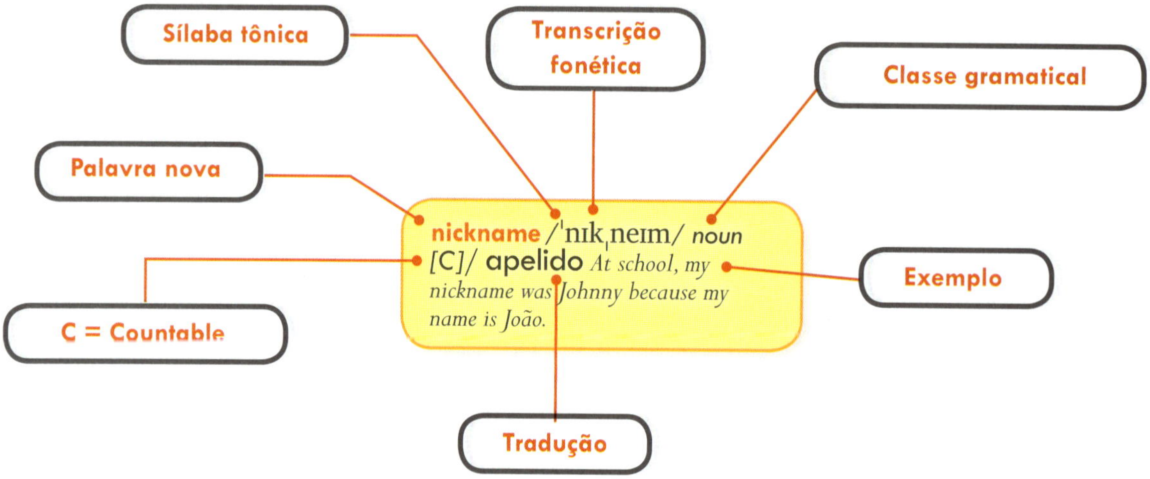

Outra boa ideia para a criação de seu glossário é relacionar, através de *mind maps*, palavras novas com aquelas que já conhece ou acabou de aprender. Por exemplo:

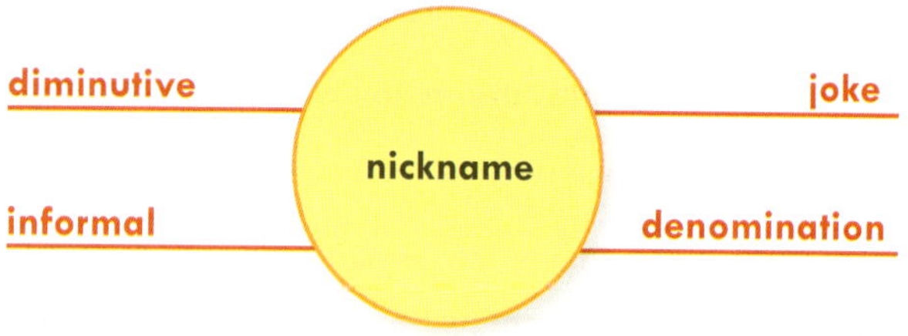

Esperamos que você possa criar um glossário que o(a) ajude a aprender inglês de forma diversificada, divertida e eficaz. Compartilhe-o, de vez em quando, com seus / suas colegas de sala. Bom trabalho!

unit 1

anthem /ˈænθəm/ *noun [C]* **hino nacional** *The first words of the Brazilian anthem are "Ouviram do Ipiranga às margens plácidas..."*

besides /bɪˈsaɪdz/ *preposition* **além de** *Who is coming to the party besides John?*

beyond /bɪˈjɒnd/ *preposition* **além** *Nobody lives beyond the river.*

border /ˈbɔː(r)də(r)/ *verb [T]* **fazer fronteira** *Brazil borders most countries in South America, except for Chile and Ecuador.*

carry /ˈkæri/ *verb [T]* **carregar** *Mark is carrying his baby in his arms.*

contemporary /kənˈtemp(ə)r(ə)ri/ *adjective* **contemporâneo, moderno** *Who is the best representative of contemporary art in Brazil?*

currency /ˈkʌrənsi/ *noun [C / U]* **moeda** *Real is the Brazilian currency.*

either... or /ˈaɪðə(r) ɔː(r)/ *conjunction* **ou... ou** *Grapes are usually either green or red.*

have /həv/ *verb* **ter** *I had a dog and a cat when I was a child.*

hanger /ˈhæŋə(r)/ *noun [C]* **cabide** *Do you prefer plastic hangers or metal ones?*

however /haʊˈevə(r)/ *conjunction* **no entanto, entretanto** *Carla is very good at English. However, she doesn't like to do grammar exercises.*

influential /ˌɪnfluˈenʃ(ə)l/ *adjective* **influente** *He is a very influential politician in his state.*

knowledge /ˈnɒlɪdʒ/ *noun [U]* **conhecimento** *My knowledge of Brazilian history is limited.*

nickname /ˈnɪkˌneɪm/ *noun [C]* **apelido** *At school, my nickname was Johnny because my name is João.*

play a role /pleɪ ə rəʊl/ *phrase* **interpretar, desempenhar um papel** *Kristen Stewart plays a very important role in the movie "Twilight." She is Bella.*

sheep /ʃiːp/ *noun [C]* **ovelha(s)** *There are ten sheep, one pig, and two horses in José's farm in Bahia.*

take advantage of /teɪk ədˈvɑːntɪdʒ əv/ *phrase* **tirar proveito de, tirar vantagem de** *People never took advantage of me because my parents were always with me.*

trade /treɪd/ *noun [U]* **comércio** *Brazil wants to promote agricultural trade with Mercosur countries.*

trivia /ˈtrɪviə/ *noun [U]* **curiosidades** *This website offers you trivia quizzes on TV shows, movies, and celebrities.*

win /wɪn/ *verb [T / I]* **vencer, ganhar** *Do you remember our first game of the competition? We won 3 – 1.*

MY GLOSSARY

MIND MAPS

unit 2

at least /eət li:st/ or /ət li:st/ *phrase* **no mínimo** *Susan reads at least twenty books in one year.*

be used to /bi ˈju:st tu:/ *modal verb* **acostumado a** *My friend is used to driving on the left. He is British.*

care about /keər əˈbaʊt/ *phrasal verb [T / I]* **importar-se com** *The only thing Peter cares about is his mother.*

child labor /tʃaɪld ˈleɪbə(r)/ *phrase* **trabalho infantil** *Stop buying things made with child labor!*

even /ˈi:v(ə)n/ *adverb* **mesmo** *It feels very hot in here, even in the winter.*

face /feɪs/ *verb [T]* **enfrentar** *Some Brazilians still face infrastructure problems.*

get-together /get təˈgeðə(r)/ *noun [C]* **reunião informal; festinha** *On Sundays there are big get-togethers in my parents' house.*

interviewee /ˌɪntə(r)vjuˈi:/ *noun [C]* **entrevistado** *The interviewee didn't feel comfortable with the questions and only answered "yes" or "no" to the interviewer.*

jail /dʒeɪl/ *noun [C / U]* **prisão; cadeia** *Karl was in jail for three years. Now he is free again.*

junk food /dʒʌŋk fu:d/ *noun [C / U]* **alimento não saudável** *My next-door neighbor loves junk food. He usually eats pizza, hamburgers, hot dogs and never eats vegetables and fruits.*

last /lɑ:st/ *verb [I]* **durar** *This film lasts two hours.*

materialistic /məˌtɪəriəˈlɪstɪk/ *adjective* **materialista, que só busca satisfação em coisas materiais** *Susan is so materialistic. The only things she cares about are money and possessions.*

miss /mɪs/ *verb [T]* **sentir falta, sentir saudades** *I miss my friends from elementary school.*

neat /ni:t/ *adjective* **organizado, arrumado** *Maria's hair is always very neat.*

nowadays /ˈnaʊəˌdeɪz/ *adverb* **atualmente** *Nowadays people are really worried about their eating habits.*

patriotic /ˌpeɪtriˈɒtɪk/ or /ˌpætriˈɒtɪk/ *adjective* **patriota** *I love my country. I celebrate my origins, my culture, and my language. I am very patriotic.*

predictable /prɪˈdɪktəb(ə)l/ *adjective* **previsível** *Most films I watch are very predictable. We know how the story goes even before watching the movie.*

realize /ˈrɪəlaɪz/ *verb [T]* **perceber** *Do you realize how inconvenient you are when I am with my friends?*

unbelievable /ˌʌnbɪˈli:vəb(ə)l/ *adjective* **inacreditável** *The opportunities Peter had in life were unbelievable. He was a very lucky man.*

MY GLOSSARY

MIND MAPS

unit 3

by accident /baɪ ˈæksɪd(ə)nt/ *phrase* **por acidente, acidentalmente** *Alexander Fleming discovered penicillin by accident.*

consultation /ˌkɒns(ə)lˈteɪʃ(ə)n/ *noun [C]* **sessão de discussão** *The president accepted to hold consultations with the population on topics like health and transportation.*

duty /ˈdjuːti/ *noun [C]* **dever** *I want to know what my duties are.*

employment /ɪmˈplɔɪmənt/ *noun [U]* **emprego** *Do you think you can find employment in a local store?*

gender /ˈdʒendə(r)/ *noun [C / U]* **gênero (masculino / feminino)** *Do you think there are many differences between the genders?*

growth /grəʊθ/ *noun [U]* **crescimento** *The rapid growth of the car industry in Brazil is fascinating.*

halve /hɑːv/ *verb [T]* **diminuir, reduzir pela metade** *Our school decided to halve the amount of water it wastes by 2020.*

inequality /ˌɪnɪˈkwɒləti/ *noun [C]* **desigualdade** *Social inequality in Brazil is still a problematic issue.*

iron /ˈaɪə(r)n/ *verb* **passar roupa** *I hate ironing at home. I prefer to do the dishes.*

join /dʒɔɪn/ *verb [T]* **juntar-se, associar-se** *I am joining a gym.*

mend /mend/ *verb [T]* **remendar, consertar** *My grandmother mended her own clothes when she was little.*

partnership /ˈpɑː(r)tnə(r)ʃɪp/ *noun [U]* **parceria** *This project is in partnership with the government and a local company.*

pick up after /pɪk ʌpˈɑːftə(r)/ *phrasal verb [T]* **organizar** *He is always picking up after his son.*

proposal /prəˈpəʊz(ə)l/ *noun [C]* **proposta** *We have some proposals for the use of the library.*

provide /prəˈvaɪd/ *verb [T]* **fornecer, oferecer, proporcionar** *We can provide a solution to your computer problems. We are the best in the market.*

solve /sɒlv/ *verb [T]* **resolver, solucionar** *How can we solve all the problems you have?*

submit /səbˈmɪt/ *verb [T]* **enviar** *Submit your proposals until next week.*

suitable /ˈsuːtəb(ə)l/ *adjective* **adequado, apropriado** *This house is suitable for a large family.*

take care of /teɪk keə(r) əv/ *phrasal verb [T]* **cuidar de** *I love you. I want to take care of you for the rest of my life.*

wife /waɪf/ *noun [C]* **esposa** *Phone your wife and tell her you are going to be late!*

MY GLOSSARY

MIND MAPS

unit 4

bin /bɪn/ *noun [C]* **lixeira** *There are recycling bins in my school.*

cluttered /ˈklʌtərd/ *adjective* **entulhado** *Her bedroom was cluttered with books and papers.*

devastated /ˈdevəˌsteɪtəd/ *adjective* **muito triste** *She felt devastated when her dog died.*

homeless /ˈhoʊmləs/ *adjective* **sem-teto** *The homeless people need shelter during winter.*

issue /ˈɪʃuː/ *noun [C]* **assunto, problema, questão** *The book that I am reading deals with environmental issues.*

life expectancy /laɪf ɪkˈspektənsi/ *phrase* **expectativa de vida** *Life expectancy at birth in Brazil is 73 years old, according to IBGE.*

measure /ˈmeʒə(r)/ *verb [T]* **medir** *What can you use to measure this room?*

melanoma /ˌmeləˈnoʊmə/ *noun [C]* **melanoma** *His melanoma was caused by the sunlight.*

petition /pəˈtɪʃ(ə)n/ *noun [C]* **abaixo-assinado** *Thousands of people signed the petition against the construction project.*

plea /pli/ *noun [C]* **súplica** *The police ignored her pleas for help.*

portray /pɔː(r)ˈtreɪ/ *verb [T]* **mostrar** *Opponents portray the president as weak.*

poverty /ˈpɒvə(r)ti/ *noun [U]* **pobreza** *Poverty is one of the most serious social problems in the world.*

probe /proʊb/ *noun [C]* **sonda** *A probe was sent into space to collect information and send it back to Earth.*

propose /prəˈpoʊz/ *verb [T / I]* **pedir em casamento** *He proposed and I said "yes."*

propulsion /prəˈpʌlʃən/ *noun [U]* **propulsão** *A jet needs propulsion to fly.*

rocket /ˈrɑkɪt/ *noun [C]* **foguete** *In the future, everyone will travel through space in rockets.*

sewer /ˈsuər/ *noun [C]* **esgoto** *The sewer system of the city is very old.*

smoke /smoʊk/ *noun [U]* **fumaça** *The air was filled with cigarette smoke.*

stinky /ˈstɪŋki/ *adjective* **malcheiroso** *You should wash your clothes, they are stinky!*

MY GLOSSARY

MIND MAPS

unit 5

accountant /ə'kaʊntənt/ *noun* [C] **contador** *I want to be either an accountant or a teacher. I'm not sure which.*

concerned /kən'sɜː(r)nd/ *adjective* **preocupado** *Mariana's mother is concerned about her performance at school.*

counselor /'kaʊns(ə)lər/ *noun* [C] **orientador, conselheiro** *You need to be very good with people to be a counselor.*

deal with /diːl wɪθ/ *phrasal verb* [T] **lidar com** *We need to deal with that problem before it gets too big.*

display /dɪ'spleɪ/ *verb* [T] **mostrar** *How do we display this information in an attractive way?*

endangered species /ɪnˌdeɪndʒə(r)d 'spiːʃiːz/ **espécies em extinção** *Pandas and other endangered species must be protected.*

excel /ɪk'sel/ *verb* [T] **sobressair-se** *Pedro is very good at languages. He excels in Spanish and French.*

figure /'fɪgə(r)/ *noun* [C] (geralmente usado no plural) **cálculo, número** *The final inflation figure is 3% for the year.*

find out /faɪnd aʊt/ *phrasal verb* [T] **descobrir** *Do you want to find out where your favorite actor / actress lives?*

handle /'hænd(ə)l/ *verb* [T] **manusear** *I don't know how to handle fragile objects very well.*

latest /'leɪtɪst/ *adjective* **último, mais recente** *Daniel Craig's latest movie is very exciting.*

make up /meɪk ʌp/ *phrasal verb* [T] **inventar, criar** *Gustavo makes up interesting stories.*

pattern /'pætə(r)n/ *noun* [C] **padrão** *We are repeating the same pattern over and over. Let's be creative.*

pitch /pɪtʃ/ *noun* [C / U] **altura do som** *The pitch of her voice is very high.*

reasoning /'riːz(ə)nɪŋ/ *noun* [U] **raciocínio** *Sara has a very interesting line of reasoning.*

reminder /rɪ'maɪndə(r)/ *noun* [C] **lembrete** *Here is a reminder that the school concert is next Saturday.*

sailing /'seɪlɪŋ/ *noun* [U] **vela (esporte)** *Sailing is an Olympic sport. Robert Scheidt and Lars Grael are Olympic sailors.*

skillfully /'skɪlf(ə)li/ *adverb* **habilmente** *She handles dangerous products skillfully.*

think through /θɪŋk θruː/ *phrasal verb* [T] **refletir, ponderar** *I don't have time to think my problems through.*

wish /wɪʃ/ *noun* [C] **desejo** *"What are your three wishes?" asked the Genie.*

MY GLOSSARY

MIND MAPS

unit 6

achieve /əˈtʃiːv/ *verb [T]* **alcançar** *Do you think it's difficult to achieve professional success?*

authorship /ˈɔːθə(r)ʃɪp/ *noun [U]* **autoria** *There is no evidence of the authorship of that book.*

awareness /əˈweə(r)nəs/ *noun [U]* **consciência** *There was a general lack of awareness about safety issues.*

confidence /ˈkɒnfɪd(ə)ns/ *noun [U]* **confiança** *She is a good student, but she doesn't have much confidence in her abilities.*

development /dɪˈveləpmənt/ *noun [U]* **desenvolvimento** *The government is promoting the development of new technology.*

effort /ˈefə(r)t/ *noun [C / U]* **esforço** *Please make an effort to be nice.*

intended audience /ɪnˈtendɪd ˈɔːdiəns/ *phrase* **público-alvo** *Our intended audience is basically teenagers and young adults.*

look for /lʊk fə(r)/ *phrasal verb [T]* **procurar** *Can you help me look for my black T-shirt?*

manage /ˈmænɪdʒ/ *verb [T / I]* **gerenciar** *Michelle knows how to manage her time very well. She is very organized.*

meaning /ˈmiːnɪŋ/ *noun [C / U]* **significado** *What is the meaning of the word "flabbergasted"? Oh, it means extremely shocked or surprised.*

own /əʊn/ *adjective* **próprio** *Everybody wants to have their own house.*

research /rɪˈsɜː(r)tʃ/ *noun [U]* **pesquisa** *We need to do more research on this specific area.*

resource /rɪˈzɔː(r)s/ *noun [C]* **recurso** *Brazil is rich in natural resources.*

seldom /ˈseldəm/ *adverb* **raramente** *Susie seldom eats at home.*

strength /streŋθ/ *noun [C / U]* **ponto forte; força** *"What are your strengths and weaknesses?" asked the interviewer.*

task /tɑːsk/ *noun [C]* **tarefa** *What do I have to do to complete this task?*

waste /weɪst/ *verb [T]* **desperdiçar** *Don't waste water! Use it rationally.*

MY GLOSSARY

MIND MAPS

unit 7

ago /əˈgəʊ/ *adverb* **atrás** *Three years ago, I worked at a bank.*

bold /boʊld/ *adjective* **negrito** *The title of the composition must be in bold letters.*

bubble /ˈbʌb(ə)l/ *noun [C]* **balão de diálogo** *A circle around the words someone says in a cartoon is a bubble.*

device /dɪˈvaɪs/ *noun [C]* **aparelho** *There is a special device for controlling the temperature in the room. It's great.*

face to face /feɪs tə feɪs/ *adverb* **cara a cara** *I prefer to say things face to face.*

feature /ˈfitʃər/ *noun [C]* **característica** *What are the features of this cell phone?*

gadget /ˈgædʒət/ *noun [C]* **dispositivo, aparelho** *This very special electronic gadget is a combination of a watch, a calculator, and a cell phone.*

get in touch /get ɪn tʌtʃ/ *phrasal verb [T]* **entrar em contato com** *We need to get in touch with them to talk about the schedule change.*

print out /prɪnt aʊt/ *phrasal verb [T]* **imprimir** *Please print that file out right now.*

request /rɪˈkwest/ *noun [C]* **pedido** *I am going to the supermarket. Any requests?*

scroll up / down /skroʊ ʌp/ /skroʊ daʊn/ *phrasal verb [T / I]* **rolar para cima / para baixo (tela de computador)** *Scroll down to see who is responsible for this website.*

shout /ʃaʊt/ *verb [T / I]* **gritar** *Don't shout! It's is very inappropriate.*

sit /sɪt/ *verb [I]* **sentar** *When I was younger, my family sat around the table and talked for hours.*

suck /sʌk/ *verb [T]* **sugar** *It is said that vampires suck their victims' blood to survive.*

the day before yesterday /ðə deɪ bɪˈfɔr ˈjestərˌdeɪ/ *adverb* **anteontem** *What did you do the day before yesterday?*

wavy /ˈweɪvi/ *adjective* **ondulado** *Peter likes to draw wavy bubbles on his cartoons.*

weak /wik/ *adjective* **fraco** *I'm feeling very weak today. I am probably sick.*

whisper /ˈwɪspər/ *verb [T / I]* *The teacher said, "Stop whispering! I can't hear you."*

MY GLOSSARY

MIND MAPS

unit 8

acronym /ˈækrəˌnɪm/ *noun [C]* **sigla** *NGO is an acronym for non-governmental organization.*

agree /əˈgri/ *verb [T]* **concordar com** *I tend to agree with your opinions quite often, but I have to disagree with you this time.*

although /ɔlˈðoʊ/ *conjunction* **embora, apesar de** *Although she has a good job, she is still unhappy. What's wrong with her?*

as long as /əz lɔŋ əz/ *conjunction* **desde que** *You can go out to play with your friends as long as you finish your homework.*

behavior /bɪˈheɪvjər/ *noun [U]* **comportamento** *Peter's behavior in school is very good.*

connectiveness /kəˈnektɪv nəs/ *noun [U]* **conectividade, conexão** *Connectiveness is a big issue for teenagers.*

etiquette /ˈetɪˌket/ *noun [U]* **etiqueta, regras de comportamento** *Etiquette is very important on formal occasions such as a job interview or a wedding.*

in fact /ɪn fækt/ *adverb* **na verdade** *I know the president of the company very well. In fact, he is my best friend.*

instead /ɪnˈsted/ *adverb* **em vez de, ao invés de** *Can I have tea instead of coffee?*

lingo /ˈlɪŋgoʊ/ *noun [U]* **língua, jargão** *Do you know all the Internet lingo such as BFF, XOXO, and B4?*

master /ˈmæstər/ *verb [T]* **tornar-se um especialista, um perito** *Is it possible to master a foreign language in one year?*

mind /maɪnd/ *verb [T / I]* **importar-se** *Do you mind if I sit here?*

require /rɪˈkwaɪr/ *verb [T]* **exigir, requerer** *Many employers require that their employees speak at least one foreign language.*

revenue /ˈrevənju/ *noun [U]* **receita, renda** *The company's estimated revenue totals $4 billion worldwide.*

sincerely /sɪnˈsɪrli/ *adverb* **atenciosamente** *He ended the email like this: "Sincerely, Mark Petersen."*

skill /skɪl/ *noun [C]* **habilidade, aptidão** *Which skills are important to master before getting a job?*

texting /ˈtekstɪŋ/ *noun [U]* **envio de mensagens de texto (SMS)** *People must avoid texting while working. It can distract you easily.*

unless /ənˈles/ *conjunction* **a não ser que, a menos que** *Unless you are a fan of that singer, his concert is disappointing.*

whether /ˈweðər/ *conjunction* **se** *I don't know whether your answer is good or not.*

MY GLOSSARY

MIND MAPS

IRREGULAR VERBS

Base form	Past	Past participle	Translation
be	was, were	been	ser, estar
become	became	become	tornar-se
begin	began	begun	começar
bite	bit	bitten	morder
blow	blew	blown	assoprar, explodir
break	broke	broken	quebrar
bring	brought	brought	trazer
build	built	built	construir
buy	bought	bought	comprar
catch	caught	caught	pegar, capturar
choose	chose	chosen	escolher
come	came	come	vir
cost	cost	cost	custar
cut	cut	cut	cortar
deal	dealt	dealt	lidar, negociar
do	did	done	fazer
draw	drew	drawn	desenhar
drink	drank	drunk	beber
drive	drove	driven	dirigir, ir de carro
eat	ate	eaten	comer
fall	fell	fallen	cair
feel	felt	felt	sentir, sentir-se
fight	fought	fought	lutar
find	found	found	achar, encontrar
fly	flew	flown	voar
forget	forgot	forgotten	esquecer
forgive	forgave	forgiven	perdoar
get	got	gotten/got	obter, conseguir
give	gave	given	dar
go	went	gone	ir
grow	grew	grown	crescer, cultivar
have	had	had	ter
hear	heard	heard	ouvir
hit	hit	hit	bater
keep	kept	kept	guardar, manter
know	knew	known	saber, conhecer
lay	laid	laid	assentar
leave	left	left	deixar, partir

Base form	Past	Past participle	Translation
lend	lent	lent	dar emprestado
let	let	let	deixar, alugar
lie	lay	lain	deitar
lose	lost	lost	perder
make	made	made	fazer, fabricar
meet	met	met	conhecer
pay	paid	paid	pagar
put	put	put	colocar
read	read	read	ler
rise	rose	risen	subir, erguer-se
run	ran	run	correr, dirigir
say	said	said	dizer
see	saw	seen	ver
seek	sought	sought	procurar
sell	sold	sold	vender
send	sent	sent	mandar, enviar
set	set	set	ajustar, marcar
show	showed	shown	mostrar, exibir
shrink	shrank	shrunk	encolher
shut	shut	shut	fechar
sing	sang	sung	cantar
sink	sank	sunk	afundar
sit	sat	sat	sentar
sleep	slept	slept	dormir
speak	spoke	spoken	falar
spend	spent	spent	gastar
steal	stole	stolen	roubar
swim	swam	swum	nadar
take	took	taken	tomar
teach	taught	taught	ensinar, dar aula
tell	told	told	contar
think	thought	thought	pensar
throw	threw	thrown	atirar, arremessar
understand	understood	understood	entender
wake	woke	woken	despertar
wear	wore	worn	vestir, usar
win	won	won	vencer, ganhar
write	wrote	written	escrever, redigir

AUDIO SCRIPTS

TRACK 2 - PAGE 23

A, B, C, D, E, F, G, H, I, J, K, L, M, N, O, P, Q, R, S, T, U, V, W, X, Y, Z

TRACK 3 - PAGE 23

a. I-N-D-I-A; **b.** S-I-N-G-A-P-O-R-E; **c.** C-A-N-A-D-A;
d. P-H-I-L-I-P-P-I-N-E-S; **e.** N-E-W Z-E-A-L-A-N-D.

TRACK 4 - PAGE 23

Presenter: This is Zack Hill at WQM, 92.5 with our daily quiz show! Today's show will be about English-speaking countries around the world! Guess the four countries we describe and win today's prize.

Country number one – This island with vast green hills is often called "The Emerald Isle." Its capital city is Dublin. The internationally famous rock band, U2, is from this country.

Country number two – It borders Mexico and Guatemala, and it's the only English-speaking country in Central America. Because it's located on the Caribbean and has a tropical climate, this country is a famous spot for ecotourism.

Country number three – It was the first African nation to achieve independence from the British colonial power. This country is often seen as a model for political and economic reform in Africa. It is famous for their colorful traditional clothes.

Country number four – In this rich Pacific nation, the landscape is diverse and can be spectacular at times. Nicole Kidman and Simon Baker are two native celebrities. The koala and the kangaroo are national icons.

The first listener to call with the right answers...(fade)

TRACK 5 - PAGE 39

Interviewer: This week we are featuring Brazilians living in other countries. Our first interview is with Eduardo Alves. When and how did you come to London?

Eduardo: I came to London for the first time in 2002 because I was unhappy with my university course and I wanted a break. I took a short course in photography and returned to Brazil. But I liked the experience so much that I came back the day after my graduation and I'm still here.

Interviewer: How did you find your first job here?

Eduardo: Humm... I worked as a cleaner in a few places. Some friends got me these jobs. When you live abroad, you meet a lot of people in the same situation and these people become your new family.

Interviewer: And what do you do now?

Eduardo: Now, I manage a restaurant in central London and work as a freelance photographer.

Interviewer: What difficulties did you have here at first?

Eduardo: At first, money. But one good thing about London is that you have different types of supermarkets with massive differences in prices. That means that even on a tight budget you can survive.

Interviewer: What are the main differences between London and São Paulo?

Eduardo: I feel completely safe in London. I take the night bus home very frequently and I don't worry. On the other hand, there's this horrible weather. London is grey, wet, and cold.

Interviewer: What do you miss most about Brazil?

Eduardo: My mother and my friends. I also miss one sunny afternoon after the other, going down to the beach, eating beans every day... so many things!

Interviewer: A message for Brazilians who want to live abroad.

Eduardo: It is amazing to live abroad and meet people from so many different places. You become more mature as a person. And of course, you have a lot of fun.

TRACK 6 - PAGE 61

Narrator: Part 1

Girl: Like many girls in Guinea-Bissau, Anita, 10, has a busy life. She gets up at six every morning to help with household chores, which is not an easy task when you share your small home with 18 other people. The structure of her house – bricks made of mud, a dirt floor, and a metal roof – reminds us that Anita lives in one of the five poorest countries in the world. There is no electricity or running water in the place where Anita lives.

TRACK 7 - PAGE 61

Narrator: Part 2

Girl: So, every morning Anita must walk to a nearby well, which was provided by UNICEF. Before this well was built, she had to walk 2 kilometers to get water. Because of that, she had little time to prepare for class. Now she arrives at class fully prepared and eager to spend her morning learning. Anita is one of the top students in the village. "I want to be a teacher, to help my mother and father," says Anita. "That would give us an easier life."

TRACKS 8 AND 9 - PAGE 77

Presenter: This is Alison Mustang at WCB. Today I am going to talk with one of the Teens Who Are Changing the World, Aisha Mustafa. Well, you don't have to speak the language of quantum physics to know Aisha's invention is cool. Let's talk to her and try to learn more about her and her idea to change the world. So, Aisha, where are you from?

Aisha: I'm from Egypt.

Presenter: Great! And how old are you?

Aisha: 19!

Presenter: So young and so smart! So, tell us, what is the problem you are worried about?

Aisha: Well, I love space and I want to be an explorer, but the problem is that fuel is too expensive nowadays.

Presenter: Why is this important?

Aisha: Because the cost of fuel limits space exploration.

Presenter: I see. And what's your idea to solve the problem?

Aisha: Well, I developed this theory about space. In my theory, space is not a vacuum. It is filled with very little particles that destroy each other.

Presenter: And how does this help space exploration?

Aisha: Well, when the little particles destroy each other, we can use them for propulsion and travel far off into space.

Presenter: Wow, that's amazing! So, if you can prove your theory, that will change everything we know about the universe, and it may be a huge innovation for the world.

Aisha: Yeah, that's what I hope!

Presenter: Congratulations, Aisha, and good luck!

Aisha: Thank you.

Presenter: This is WCB. Stay tuned for more Teens Who Are Changing the World!

TRACK 10 - PAGE 99

Presenter: Hello! And welcome to our game show! I'm your host, Jayden Price, and today we bring you a very special quiz on multiple intelligences. So let's welcome our participants... Today we have Leah Brown and her challenger, Emily Moore!

TRACKS 11 AND 12 - PAGE 99

Presenter: Hello! And welcome to our game show! I'm your host, Jayden Price, and today we bring you a very special quiz on multiple intelligences. So let's welcome our participants... Today we have Leah Brown and her challenger, Emily Moore! Let's play! Are you ready?

Participant 1 and Participant 2: Yes! Yes!

Presenter: Question 1: This great Brazilian racing driver was intelligent in many different ways, especially in terms of visual intelligence. He is still recognized for his exceptional talent and determination. Who is he: César Cielo, Gustavo Kuerten (Guga), or Ayrton Senna?

Presenter: Emily!

Participant 1: Hmm... Ayrton Senna!

Presenter: And that is... correct! Congratulations, Emily! You now have 10 points. Question 2. People who have this type of intelligence are able to control their body and handle objects skillfully. Which intelligence is it: body smart, picture smart, or word smart?

Presenter: What is your answer, Leah?

Participant 2: Body smart!

Presenter: Perfect! Now Leah and Emily both have 10 points! Now for the final question. This brilliant Brazilian athlete is the winner of two Olympic medals for sailing. He is intelligent in many ways, especially in kinesthetic intelligence. Unfortunately, because of a serious accident, he had one of his legs amputated. Who is he: Lars Grael, Bruno Fontes, or Amyr Klink?

Presenter: Sorry, Leah, but Emily buzzed in first. Emily, to win our game show today, what is your answer?

Participant 1: Hmm, this is difficult...Lars Grael?

Presenter: The answer is... correct! Congratulations, Emily! You are the winner of this episode of our game show. Thank you for participating, Leah... (fade)

TRACKS 13 AND 14 - PAGE 114

Angela: Hi everyone, my name is Angela Lee and I want to help you, high school students, to achieve success by using some study strategies.

Category 1: Managing your learning

Be in control of your study life. First of all: go to class. The number one reason students don't do well is because they skip classes. In addition, test yourself regularly and, based on the results, decide if you need to study more. It's also very important to analyze how you learn in order to make good decisions.

Category 2: Managing your time

Develop your time management skills to find time not only to study, but also to live a relaxed and healthy life. Prioritize your study tasks using to-do lists. It's also very important to study regularly and never just on the night before a test.

Category 3: Understanding visual aids

The truth is that diagrams, tables, images, and maps present information in a format that can help comprehension and increase learning. So, reading visual aids carefully can help you understand subjects more easily.

Category 4: Using web resources

Web resources can help you... (fade)

TRACKS 15 AND 16 - PAGE 137

Announcer: Are you a digital fanatic? Don't miss the chance of updating your digital supplies! Buy the latest electronic gadgets at up to 25% off. Yes, that's right, 25% off! Our entire stock of notebooks, cell phones, and LCD TVs available at up to 25% off! But this is a one-day only sale. So why pay more? Come to Jason's Electronics and get the latest models of notebooks, cell phones, and LCD TVs. This Saturday only!

TRACKS 17 AND 18 - PAGE 151

Presenter 1: Millions of people communicate daily through email, but there's a very big problem. We call it email etiquette. More and more people are finding out that what they say can become a big problem for them. Conversational emails among friends are one thing, but more people are learning to watch what they say online where manners don't apparently exist. The consequences, however, can hurt.

Presenter 2: Experts say email etiquette is a problem that no one should ignore, especially on social networking sites. It's on those sites where the number of users just keeps growing that people are using a language of their own. Here's what we're talking about: you likely know that LOL means laughing out loud, which is an easy one. But, what about ROTFL? Well, you *guessed* right if you said rolling on the floor laughing. And you're also likely to be in your teens or twenties if you know that. People this age sometimes use an online lingo that's not always OK. Some students, though, are ready to admit it's a problem. Here's what students in a campus computer lab told us.

Student 1: I find myself almost wanting to say things and then having to go back and say, "oh, wait a minute," you know? These people need to see me as an adult.

Student 2: I think most people are aware of the problem, but for the rest it can actually cost them a career, you know?

Student 3: We need to go back to good writing skills... Every time someone reads something you write, you are being judged. As email becomes the first impression, it's also what's leaving a lasting impression... (fade)

TRACK 19 - PAGE 181

See page 180.

TRACKS 20 AND 21 - PAGES 186

See page 186.

TRACKS 22 AND 23 - PAGE 192

Susan: Have you started your shopping list yet, Brian?

Brian: Not yet, Susan...

Susan: Then what about indulging those you love with amazing technology?

Brian: Why not?

Susan: Yes, listen to this. A survey of 1,500 consumers revealed that about 75% of them have at least one digital product on their wish lists... The top product is still the television. The high definition TV set is at the top of the list with 35% of consumers listing it as their dream gift. Smartphones come in second, with 30%. The tablet computer, a recent addition to the market place, is already in third place with 20%. The laptop has dropped from second to fourth place with 14% of consumers mentioning it. For all the drivers out there, the GPS was listed by 10% of the consumers. So, Brian, now you know what to put on your list.

Brian: Right!

Susan: Well, that's all for Rock's News Extra. This is Susan Bailey.

Brian: And this is Brian Jackson, heading to the stores.

REFERÊNCIAS DE SITES

Pág. 15 World-English.com <www.world-english.org/ELquiz.htm>. Acesso em 18 out. 2012.

Pág. 15 EnglishClub.com <www.englishclub.com/esl-quizzes/index.htm>. Acesso em 18 out. 2012.

Pág. 18 Listverse.com <http://listverse.com/2008/06/19/top-20-cool-facts-about-new-zealand/>. Acesso em 18 out. 2012.

Pág. 22 Abcnews.go.com <http://abcnews.go.com/Entertainment/BeautySecrets/story?id=5206738&page=4>. Acesso em 13 out. 2012.

Pág. 29 Meetup.com <www.meetup.com/Brazilian/messages/boards/thread/1400529?thread=1400529>. Acesso em 27 set. 2012.

Pág. 42 Getmacooljob.com <www.getmeacooljob.com/Job%20Descriptions/DJ%20Job%20Descriptions.html >. Acesso em 9 nov. 2012.

Pág. 43 Voices.com <http://voices.yahoo.com/interesting-volunteer-ideas-teens-want-to-1683567.html?cat=4>. Acesso em 9 nov. 2012.

Pág. 51 WorldWeWant2015.org <www.worldwewant2015.org>. Acesso em 29 out. 2012.

Pág. 53 Columbia.edu <http://www.columbia.edu/~sss31/rainbow/wife.html>. Acesso em 28 out. 2012.

Pág. 55 Ascd.org <http://www.ascd.org/conferences/Annual-Conference/ac13submit.aspx>. Acesso em 30 out. 2012.

Pág. 60 Ecotourism.org <http://www.ecotourism.org/dos-and-donts-while-traveling>. Acesso em 10 jan. 2013.

Pág. 67-68 Mom.me < http://mom.me/fun/2998-10-kids-who-are-changing-the-world>. Acesso em 22 dez. 2012.

Pág. 80 Whyzz.com <http://www.whyzz.com/what-does-a-nurse-do>. Acesso em 9 nov. 2012.

Pág. 81 Illinoisworknet.com <http://www.illinoisworknet.com/vos_portal/residents/en/Prepare/Volunteer/>. Acesso em 9 nov. 2012.

Pág. 83 <www.50waystohelp.com>. Acesso em 12 nov. 2012.

Pág. 89 Bgfl.org <http://www.bgfl.org/custom/resources_ftp/client_ftp/ks3/ict/multiple_int/questions/choose_lang.cfm>. Acesso em 17 out. 2012.

Pág. 90 Bgfl.org <http://www.bgfl.org/custom/resources_ftp/client_ftp/ks3/ict/multiple_int/results/results_action.cfm>. Acesso em 17 out. 2012.

Pág. 98 Tecweb.org <http://www.tecweb.org/styles/gardner.html>. Acesso em 18 out. 2012.

Pág. 105 Nclrc.org <http://www.nclrc.org/essentials/motivating/strategies.htm>. Acesso em 19 out. 2012.

Pág. 118 Allaboutcareers.com <http://www.allaboutcareers.com/careers/career-path-overview/tour-operators-tour-guides.htm>. Acesso em 9 nov. 2012.

Pág. 118 Education portal.com <http://education-portal.com/articles/Tour_Guide_Job_Description_and_Information_About_a_Career_as_a_Professional_Tour_Guide.html>. Acesso em 9 nov. 2012.

Pág. 118 Jobmonkey.com <http://www.jobmonkey.com/landtours/html/is_touring_for_you_.html>. Acesso em 9 nov. 2012.

Pág. 119 Cooljobs.com <www.cooljobs.com>. Acesso em 9 nov. 2012.

Pág. 120 Wisegeek.com <http://www.wisegeek.com/what-are-learning-styles.htm>. Acesso em 4 nov. 2012.

Pág. 143 Voices.com <http://voices.yahoo.com/summer-job-etiquette-teenagers-1487045.html?cat=25>. Acesso em 31 out. 2012.

Pág. 145 Classweb.gmu.edu <http://classweb.gmu.edu/tec/annotation/tacatone.html>. Acesso em 18 fev. 2013.

Pág. 145 Readwritethink.org <http://www.readwritethink.org/files/resources/lesson_images/lesson209/definition_style.pdf> Acesso em 18 fev. 2013.

Pág. 156 Allartschools.com <http://www.allartschools.com/art-careers/film-school/video-producer-interview>. Acesso em 9 nov. 2012.

Pág. 162 DoctorsWithoutBorders.org <www.doctorswithoutborders.org/news/article.cfm?id=5724&cat=field-news> Acesso em 11 out. 2012.

Pág. 163 ScienceDaily.com <www.sciencedaily.com/releases/2011/03/110314132531.htm>. Acesso em 10 jan. 2013.

Pág. 163 Skift.com <http://skift.com/2012/07/25/infographic-consumer-eating-habits-worldwide-how-hotels-capitalize-on-it/>. Acesso em 10 abr. 2013.

Pág. 164 ScienceDaily.com <www.sciencedaily.com/releases/2011/03/110314132531.htm>. Acesso em 8 nov. 2012.

Pág. 165 RebekaHelle.Hubpages.com <http://rebekahelle.hubpages.com/hub/How-To-Get-Straight-As-In-School>. Acesso em 12 nov. 2012.

Pág. 166 Pbs.org <http://www.pbs.org/wgbh/nova/physics/ fabric-of-cosmos.html>. Acesso em 19 out. 2012.

Pág. 167 Canberra.edu.au <www.canberra.edu.au/studyskills/ learning/groups>. Acesso em 15 out. 2012.

Pág. 167 TheKitchn.com <http://www.thekitchn.com/beeping-and-buzzing-at-the-table-whats-the-new-cellphone-etiquettelos-angeles-times-165282>. Acesso em 5 mar. 2013.

Pág. 168 CityOfAlamedaCA.gov <http://www.cityofalamedaca.gov/ Recreation/Teen-Job-Skills-Workshop>. Acesso em 19 out. 2012.

Pág. 170 Nasa.gov <http://imagine.gsfc.nasa.gov/docs/ask_astro/ask_an_astronomer.html> Acesso 19 out. 2012.

Pág. 171 50.usaid.gov < http://50.usaid.gov/infographic-saving-5-million-children-by-2015/plusfive-1000/?size=infographicMedium>. Acesso em 21 fev. 2013.

Pág. 172 wwf.Panda.org < http://wwf.panda.org/what_we_do/ where_we_work/amazon/>. Acesso em 19 out. 2012.

Pág. 173 Undp.org <http://www.undp.org/content/undp/en/home/mdgoverview/mdg_goals/mdg1/>. Acesso em 19 mar. 2013.

Pág174 UpAndRunning.bplans.org <http://upandrunning.bplans.com/2012/06/22/emotional-intelligence/>. Acesso em 19 mar. 2013.

Pág. 174 BusinessWire.com <http://www.businesswire.com/news/home/20120409005536/en/Time-Study-Reveals-%E2%80%9CDigital-Natives%E2%80%9D-Switch-Devices>. Acesso em 19 mar. 2013.

Pág. 175 DailyMail.com <http://www.dailymail.co.uk/news/article-2189103/Los-Angeles-Eva-Restaurant-offers-diners-discount-hand-mobile-phones.html>. Acesso em 19 mar. 2013.

Pág. 176 Guardian.co.uk <http://www.guardian.co.uk/technology/2012/oct/21/john-naughton-foursquare-social-networking>. Acesso em 19 mar. 2013

Pág. 177 VisitWoods.org <http://visitwoods.org.uk/en/visit-woods/plan-your-visit/Pages/plan-your-visit.aspx#navigationMenu>. Acesso em 19 mar. 2013.

REFERÊNCIAS BIBLIOGRÁFICAS

BAHKTIN, M. Os gêneros do discurso. In: BAHKTIN, M. Estética da criação verbal. 2a./4a. Ed. Trad. De P. Bezerra. São Paulo: Martins Fontes (1979[2003]). p. 261-306.

BAZERMAN, C. *Gênero, agência e escrita*. HOFFNAGEL, Judith C.

DIONISIO, Ângela P. (orgs.). São Paulo: Cortez, 2006.BRASIL/

SEMTEC. *Parâmetros Curriculares Nacionais: ensino médio – parte II: linguagens, códigos e suas tecnologias*. Brasília, DF: MEC/ SEMTEC, 2000. Disponível em <portal.mec.gov.br/seb/arquivos/pdf/14_24.pdf>. Acesso em 02 abril 2013.

BRASIL/SEMTEC. *PCN+ Ensino Médio: Orientações educacionais complementares aos Parâmetros Curriculares Nacionais*. Volume 1: Linguagens, códigos e suas tecnologias. Brasília, DF: MEC/ SEMTEC, 2002. Disponível em <portal.mec.gov.br/seb/arquivos/pdf/02Linguagens.pdf>. Acesso em 02 abril 2013.

BRASIL/SEMTEC. *Linguagens, Códigos e suas Tecnologias: Orientações Curriculares para o Ensino Médio*. Capítulo 3. Conhecimentos de línguas estrangeiras. 2006.
Disponível em: <http://portal.mec.gov.br/seb/arquivos/pdf/book_volume_01_internet.pdf>.
Acesso em 02 abril 2013.

BRONCKART, J. *Atividade de linguagem, textos e discursos: por* um interacionismo sócio-discursivo. Tradução de Anna Rachel Machado e Péricles Cunha São Paulo: Editora da PUC, 2003.

BULL, G.; ANSTEY, M. *Evolving Pedagogies, Reading and Writing in a Multimodal World*. Melbourne: Education Services Australia, 2010.

CRISTOVÃO, V. L. L. . Gêneros textuais e educação inicial do professor de língua inglesa. *Linguagem em (Dis)curso*, v. 10, p. 705-734, 2010.

DELORS, J. *The four pillars of Education. In: Learning: the Treasure Within, the report to UNESCO of the International Commission on Education for the Twenty-first Century*. 1996. Disponível em <http://www.unesco.org/delors/fourpil.htm>. Acesso em 02 abril 2013.

DIONÍSIO, A. Gêneros multimodais e multiletramento. In: KARWOSKI, A. M. et al. (Org.) *Gêneros textuais: reflexões e ensino*. União da Vitória: Kaygange, 2006, p. 131-144.

FREIRE, P. *Pedagogia da autonomia: saberes necessários à prática educativa*. São Paulo: Paz e Terra, 1996.

HYLAND, K. Genre Pedagogy: Language, Literacy and L2 Writing Instruction. *Journal of Second Language Writing*, n. 16, p. 148-164, 2007. Disponível em:
<http://www2.caes.hku.hk/kenhyland/files/2012/08/Genre-pedagogy_language-literacy-and-L2-writing-instruction1.pdf >.
Acesso em 02 abril 2013.

KRESS, G. *Literacy in the New Media Age*. London; New York: Routledge, 2003.

KRESS, G. Multimodality: a social semiotic approach to contemporary communication. New York: Routledge, 2010.

LANTOLF, J. P.; THORNE, *Introducing sociocultural theory. Sociocultural Theory and Second Language Learning*. Oxford: Oxford University Press, 2007.

MARCUSCHI, L.A. Gêneros textuais: definição e funcionalidade.

In: DIONISIO, A.; MACHADO, A.; BEZERRA, M. (Orgs). *Gêneros Textuais & Ensino*. Rio de Janeiro: Lucerna, 2002. p. 19-36.

MARCUSCHI, L.A. *Produção textual, análise de gêneros e compreensão*. São Paulo: Parábola. 2008.

MENEZES DE SOUZA, L. M. T. O professor de inglês e os letramentos no século XXI: métodos ou ética? In: JORDÃO, C.; MARTINEZ, J. Z.; HALU, R. C. (Orgs). *Formação desformatada: práticas com professores de língua inglesa*. Campinas: Pontes Editores, 2011. p. 279-303.

MINAS GERAIS. *Proposta Curricular de Língua Estrangeira da Rede Estadual de Ensino de Minas Gerais*. Belo Horizonte: Secretaria de Estado de Educação/MG, 2005. Disponível em <http://tinyurl.com/proposta-curricular-MG>. Acesso em 02 de abril 2013.

PALLOFF, R. M.; PRATT, K. *Collaborating online: learning together in community*. San Francisco: Jossey-Bass, 2005.

PARANÁ. Secretaria de Estado da Educação. *Diretrizes curriculares de língua estrangeira moderna para a Educação Básica*, 2008. Disponível em <http://www.diaadiaeducacao.pr.gov.br>. Acesso em 02 de abril 2013.

RIO DE JANEIRO. Secretaria de Estado da Educação do Rio de Janeiro. *Proposta Curricular: um novo formato – Língua Estrangeira. 2010*. Disponível em <http://www.conexaoprofessor.rj.gov.br>. Acesso em 02 de abril 2013.

RIO GRANDE DO SUL. *Referenciais Curriculares* – Volume 1 – Linguagens Códigos e suas Tecnologias: Língua Portuguesa, Literatura, Língua Estrangeira Moderna (Inglês e Espanhol). 2009. Disponível em <http://www.educacao.rs.gov.br/pse/html/refer_curric.jsp?ACAO=acao1>. Acesso em 02 de abril 2013.

REDE MUNICIPAL DE ENSINO DE BELO HORIZONTE. *Concepções da Escola Plural*, 3. ed. (RME-BH, 2002, p.227). Manuscrito.

SÃO PAULO. *Orientações Curriculares – Proposição de Expectativas de Aprendizagem: Ensino Fundamental II, Língua Inglesa*. São Paulo: Secretaria Municipal de Educação, 2007. Disponível em <http://portalsme.prefeitura.sp.gov.br/Projetos/BibliPed/Anonimo/ColecaoOrienta%C3%A7%C3%B5esCurriculares.aspx>. Acesso em 02 de abril 2013.

SOARES, M. *Letramento: um tema em três gêneros*. 2. ed. Belo Horizonte: Autêntica, 2003.

SOTO, U.; MAYRINK, M.F.; GREGOLIN, I. V. (ORG.). *Linguagem, educação e virtualidade: experiências e reflexões*. Editora UNESP. 2009

VYGOTSKY, L. S. *A formação social da mente: o desenvolvimento dos processos psicológicos superiores*. 6. ed. São Paulo: Martins Fontes, 1996.

WALSH, M. Multimodal Literacy: What Does It Mean for Classroom Practice? *Australian Journal of Language and Literacy*, v. 33, n. 3, p. 211-239, 2010.
Disponível em: <http://www.alea.edu.au/documents/item/63>.
Acesso em 02 de abril 2013.

WARSCHAUER, M. (2010). Digital literacy studies: progress and prospects. In M. Baynham & M. Prinsloo (Eds.), *The future of literacy studies* Houndmills, Basingstoke, UK: Palgrave Macmillan. 2010, p. 123-140.

WIDDOWSON, H. G. Teaching language as communication Oxford: Oxford University Press, 1978.

SELF-STUDY ANSWER KEY

Units 1 and 2 – 1. A J.K. Rowling; **B** Matt Groening; **C** Michael J. Fox; **D** Andrea Bocelli; **E** Charlize Theron; **F** Lionel Messi; **2. a.** is; **b.** are; **c.** is/are; **d.** is not/s; **e.** s not/s; **f.** m not; **3.** g j a d b h i c e f; **4. a.** are/play/has; **b.** is; **c.** scares; **d.** happen/keep on; **e.** don't/get; **5. a.** never; **b.** times; **c.** always; **d.** eat; **e.** don't care; **6. a.** Irish; **b.** Italian; **c.** Spanish; **d.** Colombian; **e.** Argentinian; **7.** pick up/take/water/put away/make; **Units 3 and 4 – 1.** **(X)** Students can register on the morning of the event.; **(X)** Only students from class 301 can participate in the beach cleaning competition.; **(X)** If people need information, there's a phone number they should call.; **2.** class/7-12/T-shirt/sunscreen/water; **3. a.** Don't cross; **b.** Turn down; **c.** close; **d.** don't forget; **e.** Eat/don't skip; **4. 1.** Replace/Use; **2.** Turn off/set; **3.** Don't rinse; **4.** Don't pre-heat/turn on; **5.** Recycle; **6.** Hang/get; **7.** Go; **8.** Ban/Have/take; **9.** Use/don't forget; **10.** Turn off/turn off/turn off; **5. a.** her; **b.** we; **c.** He; **d.** us; **e.** She; **f.** them; **g.** you; **6. a.** I think she's at the university. Do you need to talk to her?/We are going to start our project today. **(X)** I – she – you – her – we; **b.** Ted is a good friend, but he never returns the things he borrows. From now on I won't lend him anything. I love my books and I want to take good care of them. **(X)** he – him – I – them; **c.** I know I have met them before!/Me too, but I can't remember their names or where I've seen them . **(X)** them – me – I – them; **d.** How are you? I heard you weren't at school yesterday./But I was! The problem was that I left my essay at home and had to go back there to pick it up. **(X)** you – you – I – it; **7. a.** S; **b.** P; **c.** P; **d.** P; **e.** S; **f.** S; **8. a.** pollution; **b.** deforestation; **c.** chemical waste; **d.** public transportation; **e.** alternative sources of energy; **9.** e a c b d **Units 5 and 6 – 1.** see/hearing/language/doing/work/groups/self-study **2. b.** My gardener uses special garden tools to take care of these flowers.; **c.** I left my golf shoes back home.; **d.** Why did the Sanders bring their sweet 7-month-old baby to the party?; **e.** Andrea was wearing an amazing evening dress!; **f.** He dreamed of becoming a world boxing champion.; **3. b.** ~~bus~~ buses/articles/wardrobes/drugstores; **c.** ~~city~~ children/cities/teeth/mice; **d.** ~~radio~~ radios/heroes/potatoes/tomatoes; **4. a.** manner; **b.** place; **c.** duration; **d.** degree; **e.** time; **f.** frequency; **5.** a c e b d e **6. a.** ADJ; **b.** ADV; **c.** ADV; **d.** ADV; **e.** ADJ; **f.** ADJ; **7. a.** attend; **b.** intend; **c.** currently; **d.** relatives; **e.** private; **f.** success; **Units 7 and 8 – 1. a.** T; **b.** T; **c.** F; **d.** F; **e.** F; **f.** T; **2. b.** (X) **c.** (X) e (X); **3. b.** can use; **c.** can't talk; **d.** Can/present; **e.** can learn; **f.** can't/put/can deal with; **4.** survived/did/get/Did/send/Did/make/didn't have/tried/was/drove/texted; **5.** *Respostas possíveis.* **a.** but we went to the beach.; **b.** because she's sick.; **c.** therefore, I prefer to play volleyball.; **d.** and we're cooking.; **e.** Then, put the cake in the oven.; **6. a.** Learning; **b.** listening; **c.** doing/cooking; **d.** studying; **e.** playing; **f.** talking; **7. a.** flash drive; **b.** tablet; **c.** microwave oven; **d.** cell phone; **e.** digital camera; **8. a.** Employers/employees; **b.** Examiners/examinees; **c.** addresser/addressee; **d.** trainee/trainer.